INSIGHT *POCKET*

IBIZA

Diario de Ibiza

APA PUBLICATIONS

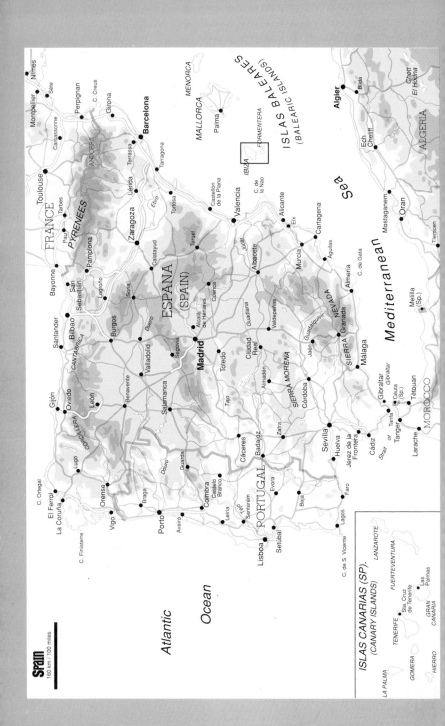

Spain
160 km / 100 miles

Atlantic Ocean

Mediterranean Sea

FRANCE
PYRENEES
ANDORRA

ESPAÑA (SPAIN)

PORTUGAL

MOROCCO

ALGERIA

ISLAS BALEARES (BALEARIC ISLANDS)
MALLORCA
MENORCA
IBIZA
FORMENTERA

ISLAS CANARIAS (SP). (CANARY ISLANDS)
LA PALMA
TENERIFE
GOMERA
HIERRO
GRAN CANARIA
FUERTEVENTURA
LANZAROTE
Sta. Cruz de Tenerife
Las Palmas

Nîmes
Montpellier
Sète
Carcassonne
Perpignan
C. Creus
Girona
Barcelona
Terrassa
Tarragona
Toulouse
Tarbes
Pau
Bayonne
San Sebastián
Pamplona
Logroño
Zaragoza
Lérida
Ebro
Tortosa
Teruel
Calatayud
Soria
Cuenca
Castellón de la Plana
C. de la Nao
Valencia
Alicante
Eix
Júcar
Albacete
Cartagena
Murcia
Aguilas
C. de Gata
Almería
Guadiana
Valdepeñas
NEVADA
SIERRA
Granada
Jaén
Guadalquivir
Málaga
Melilla (Sp.)
Oran
Mostaganem
Tlemcen
Algier
Blida
Ech Cheliff
Chott El Hodna
Palma
Santander
Bilbao
CANTÁBRICA
Burgos
Duero
Valladolid
Segovia
Alcalá de Henares
Madrid
Toledo
Tajo
Ciudad Real
Almadén
SIERRA MORENA
Córdoba
Sevilla
Huelva
Jerez de la Frontera
Cádiz
Straut of Tarifa
Tarifa
Gibraltar
Ceuta (Sp.)
Tánger
Larache
Tétouan
Gijón
Oviedo
León
CORDILLERA
Lugo
C. Ortegal
El Ferrol
La Coruña
C. Finisterre
Orense
Vigo
Braga
Porto
Aveiro
Douro
Guarda
Coimbra
Castelo Branco
Leiria
Rio
Santarém
Lisboa
Setúbal
Évora
Beja
Faro
Lagos
C. de S. Vicente
Benavente
Salamanca
Cáceres
Badajoz
Zafra
ESPAÑA

Dear Visitor!

Ibiza is not so much a place as a state of mind. A mecca for the young and fashionable ever since it became a hippie haunt in the 1960s, it offers the brightest nightlife in Europe. But while the nightclubs of the resorts grow ever more fantastic, the landscapes of the interior are almost biblical in their simplicity and just along the coast small coves lie hidden and limpid waters lap at clean beaches. Ibiza is both a hedonist's heaven and an escapist's idyll.

In these pages *Insight Guides'* expert on Ibiza will help you make the best use of your stay on this tiny island. A series of carefully crafted itineraries caters to a variety of time frames and tastes, from exploring the towns and villages to discovering the loveliest beaches. They include craft markets, churches and nightclubs and excursions by boat to neighbouring Formentera

 Barnard Collins first came to Ibiza in the wake of the hippies and the jet-set in the 1970s, when he saw it as a beacon of liberalism in a Spain still under the jackboot of Franco. Budget tourism was proliferating and Collins feared that the small island would soon be paralysed by the annual influx of holidaymakers. Thankfully, he found that, though a few areas were ruined, Ibiza largely retained its charm and even benefited from the changes. Part of Ibiza's attraction today, he claims, is that it is a true melting pot of diverse and interesting people. He says, 'The fascinating people I have met here, Ibizan and expatriate alike, have enriched my outlook on life.'

Hans Höfer
Publisher, Insight Guides

C O N T E N T S

*Pages 2/3:
Eivissa Town*

Pages 8/9:
Hedonists hang out

HISTORY

Island of Many Names

The Carthaginians called their settlement *Ibosim, Albusim* or *Ebusim*. To the Iberians it was *Ebesos*. Greek traders knew it as *Ebysos*, and they called Ibiza and Formentera together *Pitiüses*, the 'Pine Islands'. In Latin it was *Ebusus*. Arab colonisers called it *Yebisah*. In Castilian (Spanish) it is Ibiza. In Catalan, and the Ibizan dialect, which is now undergoing a revival, *Eivissa* is the name. In this book, I have used *Eivissa* to refer to the island's main town and *Ibiza* when referring to the whole island.

Roman relic from Eivissa's Dalt Vila

With names of villages, hamlets and streets, I have generally stayed with the Catalan (Ibizan) spelling. A refreshed pride in their own language, and the permission to do so since the arrival of democracy in Spain, has generated a wave of name changes, often confusing to the foreign visitor. For instance, in Eivissa's Sa Penya quarter, Calle de la Virgen has now become Carrer Mare de Deu – understandably, for Catalan people have been less impressed by Christ's virgin birth than by Mary's status as the Mother of God. Calle Mayor is now Calle d'Enmig, that is the 'street in the midst of it all'. And it certainly is.

10

First and Lasting Impressions

The fortifications surrounding the high mound of Dalt Vila (the High Town) provide visitors with the most graphic evidence of Ibiza's tumultuous history. Whether you arrive by air or sea, or approach Eivissa by road from any point of the island, it is these thick and high walls which will hold your attention, and leave a lasting impression. Two other places will also bring you into contact with Ibiza's history. They are the Museo Arqueológico in Dalt Vila and the Museo Monográfico de Puig des Molins. By world standards these are not impressive museums, but there are enough well displayed exhibits to convince you that this tiny island was for centuries of great strategic importance to different civilisations (in fact, the Museu Arqueológico has room to display only 1 percent of the items in its care). Part of the old city walls have been excavated in the foundations of the Archaeological Museum.

Ibizans Past

Archaeologists have uncovered evidence of the island's occupation from around 2000–1400BC. Unless you are a specialist, however, do not go searching for it. Ibiza's present tense is much more vivid than its past. From around 1400BC to the middle of the 7th century BC, there is an historical hiatus on Ibiza. What transpired during those almost 700 years is still a mystery. Around the middle of the 7th century, Phoenician traders, the people of Tyre,

Eivissa, topped by Dalt Vila

Fortress Eivissa

In 1554, during the last years of the reign of Carlos V, an Italian specialist in military architecture named Calvi, who also fortified the defences of Palma de Mallorca, Mahon and Barcelona, was commissioned to design new walls to protect Eivissa from attacks by Turkish raiders. Stones from the Moors' *alcázar*, sacked in the Catalan-Pisan attack of 1114, and from the medieval Christian ramparts were used in the construction. The Portal de ses Taules, the main access to Dalt Vila, was completed in 1585 during the reign of Carlos's son, Felipe II, to whom an inscription was worked into the masonry. Above the gateway is a carving of Eivissa's coat of arms. Beyond, the Pati des Armas displays an attractive combination of defensive and decorative architecture.

The walls incorporate seven *baluartes* (bastions) on which artillery was placed; last to be completed, in 1727, was the Baluarte de Sant Joan, under which is the gateway of the same name and the vehicular exit from Dalt Vila. Eivissa's walls rank as a National Monument and rate as some of Europe's finest and best preserved examples of military architecture dating from this period. Preservation and restoration work continues.

had begun calling, and staying, at Ibiza en route to their western outpost of Agadir (ancient Cádiz). The collapse of Phoenician power followed their defeat by the Babylonians in 575BC. Carthage, which had been a satellite power of the Phoenicians, assumed commercial supremacy in the western Mediterranean. Their sphere of influence included Ibiza, which experienced a wave of immigration.

Carthaginian is synonymous with Punic, the Latin term well known to all students of the Punic Wars. It is thought that Ibiza's main attraction for the Carthaginians was its lack of poisonous plants, reptiles and dangerous animals, making it the ideal place to enter the afterlife. The island became a Carthaginian necropolis. Many families sent the bodies of loved ones to Ibiza to be interred, accompanied by burial-goods which are now in Eivissa's museums. But the island's extensive deposits of salt, *ses Salines* or *las Salinas*, were also important. Salt preserved food on long sea journeys, and the Carthaginians were ever active on the sea, trading wherever they could. Ibiza made a convenient base in the western Mediterranean.

During the Second Punic War, fought between Carthage and Rome from 219-201BC, the people of Ibiza allied themselves with Carthage. There is sufficient evidence to support the view that, by then, Ibiza was truly Punic; that is, African. Even after the final conquest of the Balearic Islands by the Romans, Ibiza enjoyed a special status. Until AD79 it was a federated enclave within the Roman

Ibizan salt was once a source of wealth

Dalt Vila's northern bastion

Empire, enjoying an autonomy denied to the other Balearic islands. Its indigenous coinage was spread throughout the western Mediterranean.

Nothing much happened on Ibiza for several centuries. Latin had become the accepted language, Christianity had arrived and by the 5th century the Roman Empire was in decline. The Vandals came but were routed by Byzantine Christians. In the 8th century, Muslim Saracens began attacking the island. In the next century, the Vikings raided the Balearics. From the early 10th century to 1235, Muslims held sway on Ibiza.

Catalans and Castilians

It was a Catalan, Guillem de Montgrí, Bishop of Tarragona, who in 1235 accomplished the capture of Ibiza for the crown of Aragón and Catalunya. Rumour has it that the conquest was easy because Montgrí's forces were let in secretly by a jealous husband whose wife had been seduced by Ibiza's ruler. Land was divided amongst the Aragonese and Catalan nobility, contributors to the expedition. A semi-autonomous governing body, *la Universitat*, was established.

There was a brief period of local splendour and aggrandisement of the town. Catalan became the common language and the Ibizan dialect evolved. Ibiza fell under the influence of the new royal house of Mallorca, but not for long; in 1343 it was again subject to Aragón and Catalunya. Epidemics, including the Black Death of 1348, constant pirate raids and wars among competing monarchs made life less than idyllic. In 1403 Formentera's residents left their home, unable to protect it from pirates, and the island became a base from which Moslems harassed the rest of the Balearics.

After the 'discovery' of the Americas by Columbus in 1492, Spain's attention was diverted from its Mediterranean interests and Ibiza and Formentera passed into historical oblivion. During the War of the Spanish Succession (1702–14), Ibiza backed the Austrian claimant. The successful Bourbon, Felipe V, imposed the *Nueva Planta* decree in retribution. In 1718 Ibiza was incorporated into the Spanish province of the Balearics. Castilian culture and language took hold in a society which became a forgotten provincial backwater. Emigration was the only solution for many.

Following the Catalan conquest, the islanders were, for their better administration and protection, assigned to parishes named after saints. The people built their own churches and subsequently maintained them. Whitewashed, solid and simple, they admirably served their purposes as places of worship utilised by uncomplicated people and as sanctuaries in times of harassment by pirates. Three crosses of Calvary are the only external adornment. Parishioners exchanged news in arcaded porticos typical of all the churches and gathered in the protected inner courtyards when there was trouble. The plain interiors were decorated with such items of religious art as poor people could muster. Bells in the distinctive towers summoned parishioners to prayer and warned of impending attacks.

There were three spates of parish formation and church building: in the 14th century at Santa Eulàlia, Sant Antoni, Sant Miquel, Jesús, and Sant Jordi; in the early 18th century at Sant Josep, Sant Joan and Sant Francesc Javier (Formentera); and, after the appointment in 1782 of Ibiza's first bishop, at Sant Llorenç, Santa Agnés, Sant Augustí, Sant Mateu, Santa Gertrudis, Sant Carles, Sant Rafael, Sant Ferran and El Pilar (the last two on Formentera).

The Melting Pot

During the 1930s Santa Eulàlia and Sant Antoni felt the first stirrings of foreign interest. From the late 1950s, European artists, writers and other bohemians began to move into cottages previously occupied by fishing folk in Eivissa's Sa Penya quarter and into houses in Dalt Vila, whose original owners wanted to move to the newer, more modern areas north and west of Paseo Vara de Rey, the Eixample (Extension). These artists and craftspeople found inspiration in the island's clear light, traditional crafts, scenic beauty and isolation.

Gay people encountered a tolerance on Ibiza which they had not experienced in their own countries and arrived to settle or to return again and again as regular summer visitors. Other new arrivals, many retired and seeking a quiet life, bought *fincas* from farmers who saw no future in continuing their toil on the land and wanted, instead, apartments in town. Fishermen and farmers aban-

Roadside shrine

doned the sea and soil and became small but quickly rich players in tourism. During this period the number of restaurants, bars, nightclubs and small shops on Ibiza mushroomed.

The melting pot years of the 1950s and 60s yielded a peculiarly Ibizan society and lifestyle – laid back and tolerant, cosmopolitan yet insular, somnolent but creative. The boom years spawned their own look, *Ad Lib*, in some ways a reflection of the island's intrinsic attitude of 'anything goes'. Based on this attitude too was Ibiza's exotic style of nightlife and its scintillating disco venues, which have played such a large part in generating Ibiza's fame and fortune, and which many other summer resorts have since sought to emulate.

But despite all the changes in the last 30 years, many people on Ibiza and Formentera have remained steadfastly unchanged. Their lives unfold in the traditional way; their pleasures are family affairs, events marked on the agricultural and religious calendars which go unrecognised by the more materialistic world and by most of the tourists. With Spain's improved health and social services, life may now be less onerous than it was on the islands, but it is still not easy.

Modern Invaders

With the advent of mass tourism, the face of Ibiza has changed, and parts of the island are totally unrecognisable, transformed forever by developers. Package holiday operators clamoured for budget accommodation and ancillary offerings which local builders eagerly provided. These opportunists cared little about anything other than achieving full bookings and making a tidy profit.

At the end of the 1980s the crisis came: holiday operators could

Domestic Sugar Cubes

Architects such as le Corbusier and Sert have found inspiration in the simplicity of Ibiza's domestic architecture which is distinguished by its cubist shape. A simple dwelling may consist of just one cube; other cubes are added on as need and circumstances demand. Thick walls are whitewashed and have either no windows or very small ones which prevent the sun from penetrating the interior. A *porxet* (porch) provides shade and is also used for drying and storing vegetables and fruit. Flat roofs are supported by pine beams and made waterproof with layers of dried seaweed, charcoal and clay. Short triangular chimneys project from the roofs. An outdoor *horno* (oven) and *pozo* (well) are usually located close to the *casament* (house).

In the countryside the houses stand in a patchwork of *tanques*, small parcels of land surrounded by stone walls. A single palm, fig and other fruit trees, a small vegetable garden, aromatic bushes, colourful climbers and pots of bright flowers surround the house.

no longer assure the quantity of visitors. Hotels, apartments and all the other businesses dependent on mass tourism equally felt the pinch. Just one example of how desperate the situation had become was the offer in the early 1990s, by one of Britain's biggest holiday operators, of return flights from Britain to Ibiza plus a week's accommodation in Sant Antoni for just 9,000 pesetas, while local clients were charged 4,500 pesetas apiece for a day's excursion.

This 'bargain basement' tourism, concentrated mainly around Sant Antoni, has not affected the top end of Ibiza's tourism. The latter is represented by guests of hotels such as La Hacienda or Pike's, luxury villa owners and their tenants, and owners of fine yachts and other pleasure craft which pack the island's marinas. Ibiza continues to draw Spanish high society and political figures, rich but anonymous regulars, and ordinary people who have simply fallen in love with this beautiful island.

Environmental issues are at last being taken seriously and concerned residents and ecologists alike are doing their best to preserve the innate beauty of Ibiza. Schemes to maximise tourism are no longer allowed to go full steam ahead without concern for the environmental damage they may do. For example, to halt the gradual erosion of the island's beaches (and to increase the number of metres of usable coastline), the local government introduced boats to suck sand from the seabed and decant it on to the beaches, a scheme which has enraged ecologists concerned about the damage done to native marine species. Another conflict of interest concerns the wetland area of Las Salinas, an important habitat for flamingoes which also contains many species of insects, lizards and plants found nowhere else in the world. Whereas the central government has declared Las Salinas a protected area, the Balear government would like to urbanise it, on account of its prime position.

Sun and fun lovers on an Ibizan holiday

Historical Outline

2000 BC Food-gatherers and fishermen arrive from eastern Spain, settling in strategically situated caves and erecting stone walls. These first Ibizans work metals not indigenous to the island, evidence of foreign trade and communication.

654 Though this date was set by the 1st-century BC writer, Diodoro Sículo, as the date of the Carthaginian conquest of Ibiza, archaeological evidence supports a Phoenician presence in the 7th century BC. The Phoenicians build settlements at Sa Caleta and Puig de Vila (Eivissa), and use Puig des Molins as a necropolis for cremated remains.

573 Phoenician influence in the western Mediterranean is eclipsed by the Phocean Greeks and Carthaginians. From around 525, bodies are interred in the Carthaginian manner at Puig des Molins and there is a concurrent increase in the island's population.

450–200 Eivissa grows as an urban centre, amassing a population of 5,000, including many artisans and traders; the countryside is exploited for agriculture; oil and wine are the principal products. By the 3rd century BC, Ibiza is minting its own coinage.

200–AD75 Ibiza backs Carthage in the Punic Wars with Rome but avoids military conquest by Rome after the Carthaginians' defeat. Mallorca and Menorca are occupied by Rome in 123BC. In AD74 Ibiza becomes a municipality in the province of Tarraconensis (Tarragona).

AD75–455 Roman settlers arrive but the majority remains distinctly Carthaginian. Trade decreases and the islands drift out of the historical limelight. Vandals occupy and subjugate the islands.

535 Christian Byzantium defeats the Vandals. By 700, North Africans are raiding Ibiza and Formentera.

902–1235 The islands are incorporated into the Caliphate of Córdoba and, after its collapse, become part of the Muslim *taifa* (small kingdom) of Denia from 1015–59. From 1059–1116, they are included in the *taifa* of Mallorca. The Almoravides, the north African rulers, are replaced by their rivals, the Almohades, in 1188.

1235 Ibiza is taken on 8 August by Guillem de Montgrí, Prince Pere of Portugal and Conde Rossellón for King Jaume I of Catalunya. The island is divided into four *quartons*: Yabisa, Portmany, Balansat, Ses Salines and Santa Eulàlia. New administrative order accompanies the return of Christianity.

1276–1343 The islands are ruled by the kingdom of Mallorca.

1343–1937 A long period of historical oblivion. Political events on the mainland have little effect on the islands, a situation which prevails even after the islands become part of a Spanish province in 1718.

1937–1960 Ibiza supports Franco in the Civil War. The 'discovery' of the islands by foreign visitors is followed by growing package tourism.

1975 King Juan Carlos I becomes head of state, and steers Spain to democracy.

1983 Ibiza and Formentera become part of the Communitat Autonoma de les Illes Balears.

1991 Approval of the LEN (Ley de Espacios Naturales) designed to protect the natural reserves of Ibiza and Formentera.

1994 First official visit of the King and Queen of Spain to Ibiza and Formentera.

Ibiza and Formentera

4 km / 2.5 miles

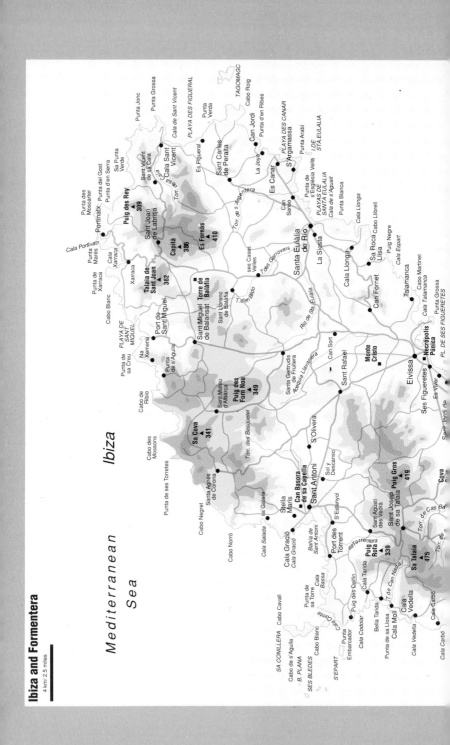

Mediterranean

Sea

Ibiza

Mediterranean Sea

Es Vedrà
▲
382

ES VEDRA

413
▲

Cala des Cubells

Cabo des Jueus

Cabo Llentrisca

Punta de Port Roig

Cala
Alegre

✈ Airport

Las
Salinas

Sa
Canal

PL. DES CODOLAR

Punta des Jondal

Sant Francesc
de Paula

Punta de sa Mata

Cala Reculta

Punta des Corb Marí

PL. DES CAVALLET

PL. DES CANAL DE S'OLLA

Punta de ses Portes

Punta de sa Rama

I. DES PENJAT

Punta de Ranxos

ESPALMADOR

Puerto del
Espalmador

Punta del Pas

Punta del
Trocadors

I. DE CASTAVI   pas   des

PL. DE SES ILLETES

Punta de Tramuntana

ESPARDELL

Punta Galera

PL. DES PUJOLS

Punta Prima

Es Pujols

Sant Ferran
de Formentera.

Cala
Savina

Sa Savina

Estany del
Peix

Estany
Pudent

Portosaler

Punta de Sa Pedrera

Punta de la Gavina

FORMENTERA

Cala Saona

Punta Rasa

Sant Francesc
de Formentera

Platja
Migjorn

PL. DE MIGJORN

Es Caló

Maryland

La Mola

*El Pilar de
la Mola*

Cala del Mort

Punta de sa Creu

Punta des Trips

Punta de sa Ruda

Punta Roja

Can Ella

Punta de S'Aguila

Torr. Saona

Cap de
Barbaria

Punta de s'Escaleta

Cabo de Berberia

You will need five or six days to follow the five day-long itineraries suggested in this book, which provide you with an in-depth look at Eivissa, an introduction to Santa Eulàlia, Sant Antoni and most of Ibiza's villages, as well as a boat tour of the coastline. There is time set aside for shopping and lazing on beaches, as well as enjoying Ibiza's exotic nightlife. In each of the itineraries, I propose restaurants, but you may want to select others from the *Eating Out* section.

If your short stay can be extended, there are more suggestions of things to do in the *Pick & Mix* options. Although the itineraries are designed to be followed explicitly, you may choose to read through all the itineraries and options and select only the activities and destinations which catch your fancy. Together, the itineraries and options are designed to provide you with a selection of all the best things to see and do on Ibiza.

Ibiza's rugged coastline

Inevitably, in a fast-changing destination such as Ibiza, restaurants, shops and nightclubs are opening and closing all the time, not to mention drifting in and out of fashion. Therefore, I have been careful to recommend only those establishments which I judged to have staying power. Of course, I may have been wrong in some cases. I both hope and believe that by the time you read this book there will be more places and amenities to attract

the discerning travellers whom I have kept in mind while research-
ing and writing.

You will want to hire a car to follow most of these itineraries
as well as most of the *Pick & Mix* options which follow. See the *Practical Information* section for pointers about car hire. (I always think
it a good idea to pack bathing gear, a change of smarter clothes
and some refreshing things such as bottled water and cologne tow-
elettes in the trunk of your hire car.) Who knows? With your nose
in this book we may bump into each other one day, sampling the
myriad delights of Ibiza and Formentera.

Elvissa, Past and Present

**Your first full day on the island introduces you to the different
parts of Eivissa town and gives you some feel for the island's
history and culture. Wear comfortable shoes with non-slip soles,
because for part of the way you will be walking up and down
hills on cobbled streets. Light and loose clothing is best and you
may want to take swimming gear.**

Start quite early by the standards of most of the island's visitors.
Get to the **Tourist Office**, at Paseo de Vara del Rey 13, by around
10am to look at any posters announcing current events and pick
up leaflets advertising what may be on during the period of your
stay. Rita, who is in charge, and her colleagues are always help-
ful. Turn right when leaving to walk along the centre of the **Paseo
Vara del Rey** which is lined by a number of colonial-style buildings with attractive façades and balconies. You will pass a statue

Day 1: Eivissa, Past and Present

320km / 0.2 miles

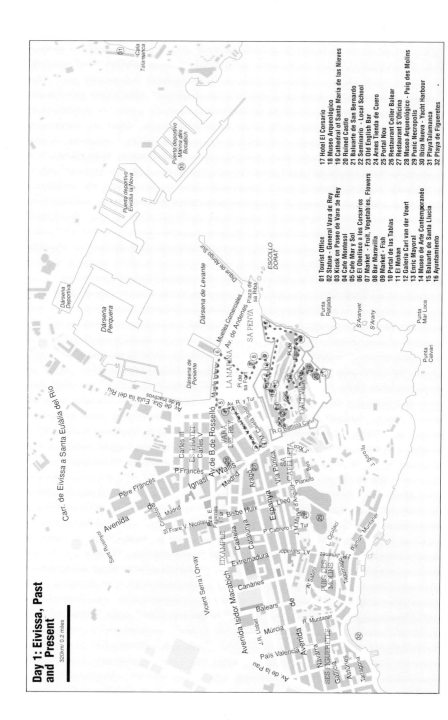

01 Tourist Office
02 Statue - General Vara de Rey
03 Kiosk on Paseo de Vara de Rey
04 Café Montesol
05 Café Mar y Sol
06 El Obelisco a los Corsarios
07 Market - Fruit, Vegetables, Flowers
08 Bar Maravilla
09 Market - Fish
10 Portal de las Tablas
11 El Mohan
12 Galería Carl van der Voort
13 Enric Mayoral
14 Museo de Arte Contemporáneo
15 Baluarte de Santa Llucia
16 Ayuntamiento

17 Hotel El Corsario
18 Museo Arqueológico
19 Cathedral of Santa María de las Nieves
20 Ruined Castle
21 Baluarte de San Bernardo
22 Seminario - Local School
23 Old English Bar
24 Arnes Tienda de Cuero
25 Portal Nou
26 Restaurant Celler Balear
27 Restaurant S'Oficina
28 Museo Arqueológico - Puig des Molins
29 Punic Necropolis
30 Ibiza Nueva - Yacht Harbour
31 PlayaTalamanca
32 Playa de Figueretes

Café Mar y Sol, ideal for people-watching

of Vara del Rey, the Ibiza-born soldier who made his name in Spain's army when the nation was losing the rest of its empire at the turn of the last century. He died fighting United States forces in Cuba. The kiosk at the end of the *paseo* sells foreign-language newspapers and magazines. Forget them – you are an escapist for a few days – and instead buy a copy of *Diario de Ibiza*, a newspaper which is handy for its detailed bus, ferry and flight timetables. During the summer months it prints a supplement in English and German. Another publication to look out for is *Ibiza Now*, in English and German.

Now cross over left towards the Café Montesol, then cross right at the traffic lights to the harbour-front **Café Mar y Sol**. This is a good place to come for a light breakfast of *café con leche* and a croissant. Sit on the terrace where the coffee costs a little more than inside because it is one of the prime people-watching spots in a town which rates people-watching as one of its main attractions. Now is also the time for a quick scan through leaflets and newspapers – and for taking in a view of activity in the bustling harbour. Bear left when leaving until you reach **El Obelisco a los Corsarios**, a monument to Ibiza's fearsome indigenous pirates, who protected the island from Barbary raiders up until the 18th century. Turn away from the harbour across Plaça de Antoni Riquer, named after one of Ibiza's most successful corsairs. Go into Calle Mar. You are now in the **La Marina quarter** where the narrow streets are lined with a variety of interesting small-shops.

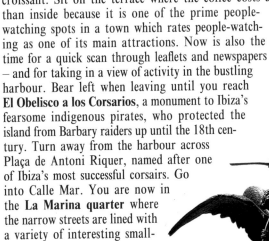

Smart boutiques attract the international visitors; simple shops cater for the needs of the locals. You may want to make a crisscrossing diversion into streets such as Sa Creu, Riambau, Bisbe Torres, Giullem de Montgrí, Bisbe Azara and Aníbal. Or leave your shopping till another time (*see Day 3, page 35*). At the end of Calle Mar turn left to reach a small, colourful market devoted to fruit, vegetables and flowers on the **Plaça de Constitució**. Continue on, with the Bar Maravilla on your left, for a quick look at the displays of local fish in the other small market.

In the Museo de Arte Contemporáneo

Return the same way to the ramp on your left which leads up to **Dalt Vila**, or the High Town. You enter it through the Portal de ses Taulas above which is Eivissa's coat of arms. There is also an inscription honouring Felipe II, Spain's king during whose reign this part of the massive defence walls and ramparts was completed. Beyond is the recently restored, colonnaded Pati des Armas and, through another archway, the picturesque Plaça de la Vila which is showing signs of neglect in parts.

Dalt Vila is undergoing an extensive programme of renovation, a process which has been plagued by financial problems and complaints of poor workmanship, especially about gas and electricity companies leaving unsightly cables exposed. There are also people who feel that some of Dalt Vila's great charm will be lost if it is prettified too much, then loses its local families and becomes merely an enclave of wealthy people who can afford the higher prices of improved housing.

Not to be missed on the Plaça de la Vila is the **Galeria Carl van der Voort**. One of Ibiza's leading art galleries, this is run by Kati Verdera who was also responsible for the revival of the Contemporary Arts Museum. (See the *Shopping* section, *page 71*.)

Leave the square by the rising road on the left and turn sharp left again as soon as you can. Ahead is the **Museo de Arte Contemporáneo** (10am–1.30pm and 5–8pm; Saturday 10am–1.30pm, closed Sunday and public holidays). It is located in an attractive old building and

In the produce market

Art on the street

has temporary exhibits by Spanish and foreign artists upstairs. Downstairs there is a permanent display of oil paintings. From the balcony you have good views of Dalt Vila's eastern ramparts and the crumbling Sa Penya quarter, where many of Eivissa's gipsy families live.

Exit from the museum to the left and on to the top of the wall towards the **Baluarte de Santa Llúcia** (bastion). There are extensive views over Sa Penya and La Marina to the harbour and newer parts of Eivissa. A ring of low hills lies beyond. Turn around and there are the white buildings of Dalt Vila, topped by its cathedral of amber stone. It is likely you will want to take a few pictures here. Continue around, with the sea far below the cliffs on your left. Soon on your right you will see the tiled cupolas of the Iglesia de Santo Domingo. Go up some steps to the **Plaça Espanya**. The big white building is the **Ayuntamiento** (Town Hall) which was built in the 17th century as a Dominican convent. See if there are any posters advertising forthcoming recitals in its delightful cloister or small chapel.

Just beyond the square turn left up steps into Calle Santa María. Soon on your right is the entrance to **El Corsario**, a very welcoming hostelry to which I suggest you return for a drink later. Continue up the steep alley, through an archway and then left. Here in **Calle Mayor** are most of the best remaining examples of solid looking noble houses which the town's leading citizens raised for themselves. Some date from the 15th century; one such, at No 18, has been earmarked to become a museum for the work of two of Ibiza's most acclaimed artists, father and son Narcís Puget i Viñas (1874–1960) and Narcís Puget i Riquer (1916–83).

You pass a variety of art and souvenir shops before entering the Plaça de Catedral. There are more good views on your left; then head for the **Museo Arqueológico de Dalt Vila** (10am–1pm and 4–7pm, closed Sunday and public holidays). It is small and its exhibits are

Calle Sant Josep

limited but they are interesting for tracing all historical periods of Ibiza and Formentera – prehistoric, Phoenician, Carthaginian, Roman, Moorish and Catalan. Sections of the old city wall have been excavated in the basement of the musuem.

Adjoining the museum is the **Antigua Universitat**, home to the islands' governing body during the period of Catalan rule. The cathedral (daily 10am–1pm) was built in the 13th century situated on a site where Punic and Roman temples and a mosque had previously been erected. After extensive renovation it is now of only limited architectural interest but it does reveal the pleasing simplicity typical of Ibizan architecture. There is a small treasury of religious art and objects.

The **Castell** was successively changed over the centuries to serve the different defence needs of various rulers. It last saw remodelling in the 18th century and has been allowed to fall into ruin since. Between the Cathedral and the Castell an alley leads to the **Baluarte de San Bernardo**. From here, the view is across to Figueretes, Platja d'en Bossa and the south of the island. To the southeast, the outline of Formentera is usually visible.

The **Palacio Episcopal** dates from the 13th century and completes the set of buildings around the Plaça de Catedral. Note its fine Gothic portal. Now return to **El Corsario** for a drink after what has probably been thirst inducing sightseeing. Order your drink

Iglesia de Santo Domingo, notable for its tiled cupolas

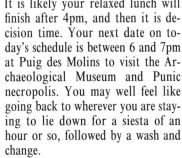

Local boutique

on the terrace from which vantage there are grand sweeping views across Eivissa and beyond. Unfortunately, the restaurant here is not open for lunch but I do recommend it for dinner (see *Eating Out, page 81*).

Fully refreshed, take the steps down on the left and bear left at the bottom. On the right is the **Seminario**, whose tower is one of the few remaining structures dating from the Moorish period. Go right into the stepped street, Calle Conquista. Around here you see some of the typical whitewashed houses of Dalt Vila. Go left into **Calle Sant Josep**. At No 9, the woman who usually sits in the doorway of her tiny shop doing embroidery sells odds and ends of needlework for women. Down more steps and you are in Plaza del Sol, a gathering place for local families. **Arnes Tienda de Cuero**, Calle Sant Antoni 9, on the right of the square, has a good selection of leather craft products.

Leave the plaza through the tunnel of Portal Nou, one of the three gateways through Dalt Vila's thick walls. Turn left at the exit and continue straight ahead across Paseo Vara del Rey into Avenida Ignasi Wallis. At No 18 on the right, the **Celler Balear** is a cool place for lunch. Service is attentive, prices are moderate and the food is unfussy and tasty. An Ibizan salad followed by a paella is one recommendation. Use the telephone at the bar to make a booking for dinner at around 10pm on the *terazza* at **Restaurant S'Oficina** (tel: 30 00 16 or 30 13 17). It is likely your relaxed lunch will

finish after 4pm, and then it is decision time. Your next date on today's schedule is between 6 and 7pm at Puig des Molins to visit the Archaeological Museum and Punic necropolis. You may well feel like going back to wherever you are staying to lie down for a siesta of an hour or so, followed by a wash and change.

If you want to persevere, take the short walk back to the quay in front of the Café Mar y Sol. Small ferry boats leave on the hour and half hour for the 10-minute trip to **Talamanca beach**, stopping at Ibiza Nueva yacht harbour on the way. They return at 10 and 40 minutes past the hour. The return fare is only 200 pesetas. You will get some bracing fresh air and fine views of Eivissa, as well as

El Palio in Calle Sant Josep, known for home décor

seeing one of the two beaches closest to town. Perhaps, have a swim. On your return, take a taxi from the rank at Mar y Sol and ask for the **Museo Monográfico Puig des Molins** (also known as Museo Monográfico de Puig des Molins), a 5-minute ride. This museum displays grave-goods from the hill which served as the town's necropolis from around 650BC until the 1st century AD. Many of the 3,000 tombs were later raided but there still remains an interesting collection of everyday and decorative objects from the Carthaginian period. Fewer finds document the earlier Phoenician and later Roman periods. Pride of place is given to a terracotta bust of the goddess Tanit which has been dated as 5th- to 4th-century BC. You will be taken to see one of the tombs.

Turn left on leaving the museum, left when you reach Avenida de Espanya and first left again down Calle Ramón Muntaner. Your 10-minute walk will have brought you to **Playa de Figueretes**, Eivissa's other beach and package holiday territory. Do as many others will be doing at this time of the evening: take a *paseo* along the promenade and then have a leisurely cocktail or beer at one of the bars.

Remember your booking for dinner at **Restaurant S'Oficina**. You can take a taxi from the rank behind the Figueretes promenade. Basque cooking has the highest reputation among Spain's regional cuisines and at S'Oficina they do it well for about 5,000 pesetas per person for a three-course meal with wine. It will be after midnight when you finish your meal – too early for bed by Ibizan rules, although you have just had a long day.

Back from the beach

Santa Eulàlia and the Northeast

You have quite a busy day ahead visiting Santa Eulàlia, the island's third largest and most sedate town, seeing quite a bit of the east and north coasts, having a swim and taking a short boat trip. You will be driving through delightful countryside to sleepy villages and hamlets, and if it is Wednesday or Saturday, you can also take in a 'hippy market'. Get to the hamlet of Jesús by around 10am.

Nuestra Señora de Jesús

Off on the right of the Eivissa to Santa Eulàlia (via Cala Llonga) road an archway leads to **Nuestra Señora de Jesús**, your first sight of a typical Ibizan church. Simple and solid, Ibiza's churches were built by their parishioners to be places of worship as well as refuges when pirates threatened. This was one of a number erected in the first spate of church building during the 15th century and it is more notable for containing the island's most prestigious work of religious art, a **Gothic retablo** (altar screen) by Rodrigo de Osona.

Return to the intersection and turn right. The road starts rising across the Serra de Balansat hills. A quarry's ugly scar mars the landscape on the right. After 5km (3 miles), you pass the 27-hole **Club de Golf Ibiza** (tel: 19 60 52). Three kilometres (1¾ miles) on, turn right to Cala Llonga. You will have your first sight of a place where some cheap and nasty property development has damaged an idyllic location, in this case the beachhead and sides of what is a beautiful mini-fjord. You may not want to linger. Go back to the main road, turn right and, going down hill past pinewoods and fields, after 4km (2½ miles) there

Ad Lib fashion

is the intersection with the main Eivissa–Santa Eulàlia road. Turn right and some 500m (¼ mile) on, across the island's only river, take a sharp left, uphill turn to **Puig d'en Missa**.

The domed church is a 14th-century remodelling of a mosque and, apart from Eivissa's cathedral, is the most impressively situated of the island's churches. Whitewashed, flat-roofed houses lie below.

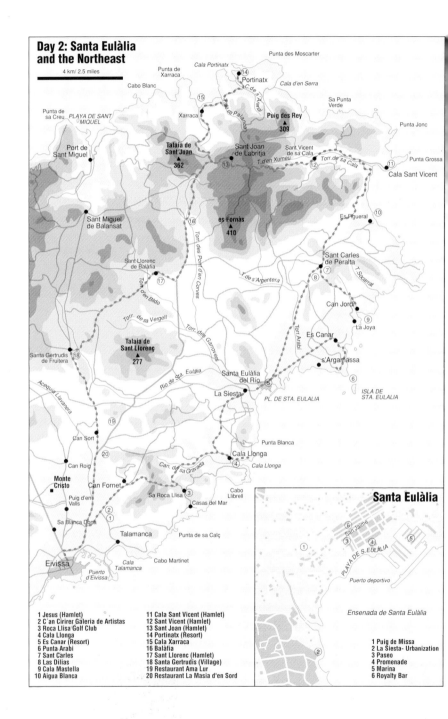

Day 2: Santa Eulàlia and the Northeast

4 km/ 2.5 miles

Punta des Moscarter
Cala Portinatx
Punta de Xarraca
Portinatx ⑭
Cala d'en Serra
Cabo Blanc
C. de s'Arad
⑮
Sa Punta Verde
Punta de sa Creu
PLAYA DE SANT MIQUEL
Xarraca
de sa Palanca
Puig des Rey
309
Punta Jonc
Port de Sant Miguel
Talaia de Sant Joan
362
Sant Joan de Labritja
Sant Vicent de sa Cala
Torr. de sa Cala
⑪ Punta Grossa
⑬
T.d'en Xumeu
⑫
Cala Sant Vicent
Sant Miguel de Balansat
⑯
es Fornàs
410
Es Figueral
⑩
Sant Carles de Peralta
⑦
Sant Llorenç de Balàfia
Torr. des Port d'en Corves
T. de s'Argentera
T. Socarrat
⑧
Torr. d'en Bildo
Can Jordi
⑰
Torr. de sa Vergell
La Joya
⑨
Es Canar
Torr. dels Garroves
Talaia de Sant Llorenç
277
Torr. Arabí
Santa Gertrudis de Fruitera
⑱
s'Argamassa
Acequia Llavanera
Rio de Sta. Eulàlia
Santa Eulàlia del Río
⑤
⑥
ISLA DE STA. EULALIA
La Siesta
PL. DE STA. EULALIA
⑲
Can Sort
Punta Blanca
⑳
Can Roig
Cala Llonga
Monte Cristo
Can Fornet
Can. de sa Gravada
④
Cala Llonga
Puig d'en Valls
②
Sa Roca Lisa
③
Cabo Llibrell
①
Casas del Mar
Sa Blanca Dona
Talamanca
Punta de sa Calç
Eivissa
Cala Talamanca
Cabo Martinet
Puerto d'Eivissa

1 Jesus (Hamlet)
2 C´an Cirirer Galeria de Artistas
3 Roca Lisa Golf Club
4 Cala Llonga
5 Es Canar (Resort)
6 Punta Arabi
7 Sant Carles
8 Las Dilias
9 Cala Mastella
10 Aigua Blanca

11 Cala Sant Vicent (Hamlet)
12 Sant Vicent (Hamlet)
13 Sant Joan (Hamlet)
14 Portinatx (Resort)
15 Cala Xarraca
16 Balàfia
17 Sant Llorenc (Hamlet)
18 Santa Gertrudis (Village)
19 Restaurant Ama Lur
20 Restaurant La Masia d'en Sord

Santa Eulàlia

San Jaime
⑥
③
④
⑤
①
PLAYA DE S.EULALIA
Puerto deportivo
②

Ensenada de Santa Eulàlia

1 Puig de Missa
2 La Siesta- Urbanization
3 Paseo
4 Promenade
5 Marina
6 Royalty Bar

Follow the signs to the recently inaugurated **Ethnological Museum of the Pitiusan Islands** (11am–1pm and 5–8pm, closed on Sunday and Monday morning), housed in a traditional Ibizan *finca* (estate). The Museo Etnológico has recovered artefacts relating to the island's rural past and on display you will find agricultural implements, traditional clothing and jewellery, a wine cellar housed in a cave, a kitchen with traditional utensils and an old oil mill. Walk around to take in views across Santa Eulàlia and the extensive La Siesta and Montañas Verdes urbanisations. There is also a haunting cemetery which is usually open for viewing. Driving back down, turn left when you reach the main street. Park as soon as you see a space and walk to the *paseo* which leads from the main road to the sea. Arts and trinkets stalls should be open. Take a stroll among them and along the beachside promenade which is lined with apartment blocks, hotels, cafés and restaurants. At the northern end is the new marina. The **Royalty Bar**, back at the corner of the main street and Plaça de Espanya, is where many residents and regular visitors do their daytime chatting and people-watching. After some refreshment, head out of town, northeast along the main street. Just on the outskirts, the road forks, offering alternatives which vary depending on the day.

If it is Wednesday, take the right fork and continue for 3.5km (2 miles) to Es Canar, a resort popular with young families. Take the road around to the right past the small port and you will soon see signs to the **Hippy Market** at **Punta Arabi** (see *Pick & Mix Option 1, page 47*). Spend around an hour at the market, return to Es Canar and, just outside the resort, take a road on the right which runs for 3km (1¾ miles) through wooded hills to Sant Carles. The remains of lead mineworkings can be seen on the right after joining the main road. Any other day, take the left fork outside Santa Eulàlia for the 6.5-km (4-mile) straight run to **Sant Carles**, where many hippies and alternative lifestylers, have settled. Here is the typical church, this one especially liked for its portico, and **Papillon**, a small boutique selling locally designed clothing for women. If it is Saturday, stop at **Las Dalias**, on the left just before entering the hamlet (see *Pick & Mix Option 1, page 49*).

Hippy Market at Punta Arabi

The small village of Santa Gertrudis

It is getting to be around lunchtime now. You may want to eat at **Las Dalias Restaurant**. **Anita's** (also known as Pep Beret), at the intersection in the centre of Sant Carles, is a popular bar with good *tapas*. The early hippies first made it their haunt. But the objective today is to try for a table at the *merendero* on the water's edge of **Cala Mastella**, known locally as Chiringuito de Bigotes, an allusion to the owner's moustache, where the dish of the day will be fish caught earlier by Señor Ferrer. His boat is moored in the tiny port. To get to Cala Mastella, take the road opposite Anita's which is signposted Cala Llenya, and 2km (1¼ miles) on turn left, left again at the next junction and very soon left onto a dirt road, signposted Cala Mastella. Park at the beach and walk over the rocks on the left. If you cannot get a table, or the fish has run out, you may want to try to make a reservation at this delightful spot for another day, and go back to Las Dalias or Anita's for the time being. But do have a swim while you are here; not from the beach but from the port wall or the rocks beyond.

Back in Sant Carles, take the road to Cala Sant Vicent. For some 4km (2½ miles) you pass by swathes of olive and carob trees. On the right is a small road to **Aigua Blanca**, one of the island's two nudist beaches. Do not bother to make the detour as it is a narrow strip of beach and not very pleasant. Continue through pinewoods for about 2.5km (1½ miles) and, where the road bends sharply to the left, there is a high view into Cala Sant Vicent. Another once beautiful *cala*, since overwhelmed by low-quality tourist development, it is best seen from a distance. Continue down and left at the T-junction. For about 3km (1¾ miles), you drive through a valley of fruit trees, oleander bushes and pine-covered slopes. After the tiny hamlet of **Sant Vicent**, the road

Sundown, Dalt Vila

twists up for some 6km (3¾ miles) through pine-clad hills and you begin to understand why the Greeks named Ibiza and Formentera the *Pitiüses*, or Pine Islands. Fulfilling escapist dreams, *fincas* lying in the folds of distant hills look like white sugar cubes.

Shortly after the hamlet of **Sant Joan**, turn right for a twisting drive between high hills until you start getting sea views again. The town of **Portinatx** is 8km (5 miles) from the turnoff. The resort development leaves something to be desired but there are three attractive beaches. Hire a motorboat or Zodiac from Playa la Port or Playa S'Arenal Petit to explore for an hour or so **Cala d'en Serra** and the uninhabited coastline to the east. And take a refreshing dip! It will be around 7pm and time to make a reservation for dinner at 10pm. Lunch will have been inexpensive; tonight dinner is going to cost between 6,000 and 8,000 pesetas per person. **Restaurant La Masia d'en Sord** (tel: 31 02 28) is an attractively converted *finca* with a delightful garden terrace. The menu is international with some local specialities. In elegant surroundings, **Restaurant Ama Lur** (tel: 31 45 54) offers Basque *nouvelle cuisine* of a high standard and its terrace is delightful.

Leave Portinatx and after about 3km (1¾ miles) watch for the turning right to **Cala Xarraca**. Pop down for a quick look at this pretty cove. Back on the main road, at the junction turn right in the direction of Eivissa. Five kilometres (3 miles) on, turn right at a signpost to Sant Llorenç and take the first dirt track to the right. Park where you can when you come to the fortified hamlet of **Balafia**, a step back in time and almost a step into Africa. This unchanged cluster of flat-roofed houses and defensive towers shows all the signs of its Moorish origins. Continue through another typi-

Flower-power night at Pacha

cal hamlet, Sant Llorenç – church and bar – and then for 6km (3¾ miles) along a peaceful road through farmland where the rich, red soil will look even redder in the evening light.

Cross the main road into **Santa Gertrudis**. Look in at its small shops and don't miss **Punta A** where Montserrat Borrell arranges shows by contemporary Spanish artists. The hamlet's bars, such as **Bar Costa**, are popular with expatriates. Join them for a drink and, perhaps, some conversation. You may want to go back to wherever you are staying for a shower before dinner.

Restaurant Ama Lur is 3km (1¾ miles) from here the road to Eivissa, on the left after the first crossroads. **Restaurant La Masia**, is 2km (1¼ miles) further on, also on the left. Enjoy a fine meal. Then think about going to bed but don't do it. **Pacha disco** is only 5km (3 miles) away. Take the last exit around the first traffic island at the entrance to Eivissa. A few hours here will be a sparkling end to your second day.

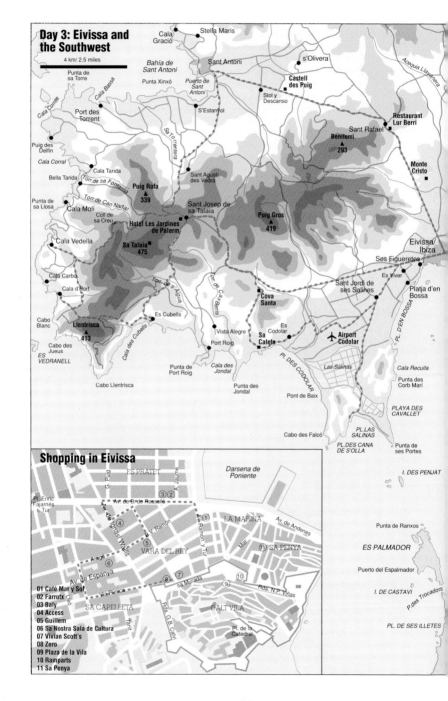

Day 3: Eivissa and the Southwest

4 km/ 2.5 miles

Cala Graciò
Stella Maris
Bahía de Sant Antoni
Sant Antoni
s'Olivera
Acequia Llavanera
Punta de sa Torre
Cala Bassa
Punta Xinxò
Puerto de Sant Antoni
Castell des Puig
Stol y Descanso
Cala Comte
Port des Torrent
S'Estanyol
Restaurant Lur Berri
Sant Rafael
Puig des Delfin
Sa Torrentera
Beniferri
293
Monte Cristo
Cala Corral
Cala Tarida
Bella Tarida
Torr. de sa Fontassa
Sant Agusti des Vedra
Punta de sa Llosa
Torr. de Can Nadal
Puig Rota
339
Cala Molí
Coll de sa Creu
Sant Josep de sa Talaia
Puig Gros
419
Hotel Les Jardines de Palerm
Cala Vedella
Sa Talaia
475
Eivissa/ Ibiza
Ses Figueretes
Cala Carbò
Torr. de s'Aigua
Torr. de C'a.s Berris
Es Viver
Sant Jordi de ses Salines
Platja d'en Bossa
Cala d'Hort
Cova Santa
PL. D'EN BOSSA
Cabo Blanc
Llentrisca
413
Es Cubells
Vista Alegre
Es Codolar
Es Caleta
Sa Caleta
Airport Codolar
Cabo des Jueus
ES VEDRANELL
Cala des Cubells
Port Roig
Punta de Port Roig
Cala des Jondal
PL. DES CODOLAR
Las Salinas
Cala Recuita
Cabo Llentrisca
Punta des Jondal
Pont de Baix
Punta des Corb Mari
PLAYA DES CAVALLET
Cabo des Falcó
PL. LAS SALINAS
PL. DES CANA DE S'OLLA
Punta de ses Portes

Shopping in Eivissa

ES PRATET
G. Puig
Darsena de Poniente
Pl. Enric Fajarnés i. Tur
Av. de B. de Rosselló
LA MARINA
Av. de Andenes
Av. de Ignasi Wallis
Ramon y Tur
Ramon y Tur
SA PENYA
VARA DEL REY
Aragó
Mar
sa Murada
Av. de Espanya
Rda. N.P. Viñas
SA CAPELLETA
Vía Púnica
Rda. G.B. Calvi
DALT VILA
Tarré
Pl. de la Catedral

01 Café Mar y Sol
02 Farrutx
03 Baly
04 Access
05 Guillem
06 Sa Nostra Sala de Cultura
07 Vivian Scott's
08 Zero
09 Plaza de la Vila
10 Ramparts
11 Sa Penya

I. DES PENJAT
Punta de Ranxos
ES PALMADOR
Puerto del Espalmador
I. DE CASTAVI
P. des Trocadors
PL. DE SES ILLETES

DAY 3

Elvissa and the Southwest

This is an exercise in self-indulgence. Get up a little later, visit the shops in Eivissa's more modern sector, have lunch at a beach bar and laze on the beach. Then, take a leisurely drive to see places in the southwest of the island. Get a glimpse of much maligned Sant Antoni and stop to shop in villages on the way. Then, there is more shopping in the old quarters of Eivissa, followed by dinner in Sant Rafael or Dalt Vila.

Start the day off again at **Café Mar y Sol** in Eivissa, where you are becoming almost a regular. At around 11.30am, you should be paying your bill. In one and a half hours the shops will start closing. If you buy anything of value, get a detailed receipt and tell the shop you will pick up your purchases later. It is not wise to leave valuable items in your car, even in a locked boot. Cross over to **Avenida B de Roselló**, the street leading west away from the harbour. On its north side, at the corner of the first street, are two shops in which you may want to linger. **Farrutx** carries women's leatherwear, including handbags, shoes and belts; **Galy** also has men's fashions with labels such as Adolfo Domínguez, Cerruti and Giorgio Armani. Other shops along this street may take your fancy. Turn left at Avenida de Ignasi Wallis. On the next corner is **All Access**, a men's boutique.

Go along Calle Pere de Portugal and first right into Calle Vicente Cuervo. At No 9 on the right, **Guillem** is a good jewellery shop with traditional and modern designs. You can also buy Majorica artificial pearls from Mallorca which are incorporated in tasteful necklaces, earrings and brooches. Walk west along **Calle Vicent Ramón**, crossing over Ignasi Wallis to Calle Aragó. There may be a good art exhibition at the **Sa Nostra Sala de Cultura**, No 11 on the left. Continue along Calle Aragó to the first road left; cross Avenida de Espanya and go first left into **Via Púnica**. You will be passing a variety of shops, usually cheaper than their counterparts in the more fashionable parts of town. Go straight across at the intersection to see **Vivian Scott's** antiques and home décor display in Calle Jaume I. By now it will be about 1pm, probably hot and definitely time for a quick drink and *tapas* (snacks). Go upstairs at **Quefa**, a German charcuterie and delicatessen in Calle M Caietá Soler, the next street north.

Eivissa's more modern sector

Then it is back to your car.

Follow signs to the *aeropuerto*, leading you southeast out of town. Beyond the hamlet of Sant Jordi, take the left fork, signposted Sa Canal. After 4km (2½ miles), there is a left turn to **Es Cavallet beach**. Or continue between the salt pans until a traffic island, where you exit on the left to reach the parking area for **Las Salinas beach**. Both beaches are delightful, have good *merenderos* and are very much 'in'.

Es Cavallet is the official nudist beach and it is almost obligatory to strip totally. Gay people gather at the beach's southern end. Many people go nude at the eastern end of Las Salinas and in secluded coves further along. Whichever beach you choose, enjoy a simple lunch at a *merendero*, a bottle of wine and pass out – or be madly active, if you like. I prefer to watch the accomplished bat and ball players at Las Salinas who seem able to play for hours on end. At around 5pm, you should be back in your car, heading towards Eivissa but, some 5km (3 miles) from either beach, turn left at the airport junction. Bear right at the bar opposite the runway. The many windmills around here pump water from the underground supply which has suffered depletion and subsequent contamination by salt water.

At the next junction go left and immediately right. Soon you reach the picturesque cove of **Sa Caleta**, where fishing folk have their huts. Along a quiet road, you then pass through a rural landscape to reach the main Eivissa to Sant Josep road, where you turn left. Five minutes later you are in the pristine village which lies below Sa Talaia, the island's highest eminence at 475m (1,558ft). Park near the church, if you can, and at least have a look at its attractive porch. Pop into the shops of **El Palio** (antiques, ceramics and other home décor pieces) and **Bernat Vinya** (embroidery and other needlework). You can slake your thirst at the bar next to the latter which sells freshly squeezed and refreshing fruit juices.

If you have about an hour and a half in hand you can now take the road signposted **Es Cubells** to meander through a rural land-

Las Salinas beach

scape to this hamlet, which sits above a rugged coastline where quite a few luxury villas have been built. Leaving Es Cubells, quite soon turn left to take a gravel road in good condition to **Cala d'Hort**. Along the way you get views of the pinnacle of Es Vedra, which rises 382m (1,253ft) from the sea and is the subject of numerous legends. Cala d'Hort has a curving bay, pleasant beach and has not been much developed. Its beach restaurants are popular with islanders.

Take care on the road to **Cala Vedella**, a deeper cove where there has been more tourist development, including some smart villas hidden among the pines. On the easy road back to Sant Josep

look out for a sign on the right leading to Sa Talaia and, if it is a fine, clear day, drive up this narrow, twisting At the top wonderful views extend across the whole island, and beyond.

At the junction of the Sant Josep/Sant Antoni road, go left. On this 8-km (5-mile) drive through a rural landscape down to **Sant Antoni**, the resort can often be glimpsed in the distance. That is quite likely how you would like to have left things when you get into the ugly urban sprawl along the south side of its wide bay. If this is the case, turn right onto the Eivissa road at the T-junction traffic lights. On the other hand, while you are here, why not take a brief look at a place which has become a legend on account of the bad taste

Souvenir shopping

and bad behaviour of its young foreign visitors? There has been excessive, low-quality building and some streets have been turned into garish passages lined by trashy souvenir shops and bars and restaurants selling home-from-home food and beer. But I still maintain that Sant Antoni does not fully deserve all of its adverse publicity; there are coastal places in Britain, Italy and elsewhere which display far less charm (see *Pick & Mix Option 7, page 61*).

Back on the road, you soon turn off left into **Sant Rafael**, a village with a number of *cerámicas*. Shortly after the turnoff, on the left, is **Es Moli**, the shop and studio of Julio Bauza, a most accomplished craftsman. Try to see his work and visit other *cerámicas* which may be open.

This evening we return to Dalt Vila to dine, so browse through the list the recommended restaurants (see the *Eating Out* section, *page 81*) and book a table for later on. By now it should be around

Sant Rafael potter at work

8pm. You may be feeling sticky and want a quick wash and change before embarking on the evening, so dash back to wherever you are staying. But try to get to Dalt Vila as soon as you can.

In Dalt Vila's Plaça de la Vila you may want to re-visit the Galeria Carl van der Voort which we dipped into during the Day 1 itinerary (*see page 24*). You can also pop into **Marfil**, on the left of the road leading upwards out of the square, which is devoted to jewellery, etc made from coral. Walk on to the ramparts to get a view of the twinkling town below and the rising old town and floodlit cathedral. Then, head down towards bustling **Sa Penya**, through the Portal de ses Taulas, down the ramp and, passing the market on your left, continue straight ahead.

Spend the time left before dinner wandering the shopping alleys, where you will find a range of upmarket and innovative boutiques. In recent years, under the auspices of the designer Cristina Buscetta, a group of local designers has broken away from the white flowing style which has been the signature of Ibiza's fashion for so long. Do not miss shops such as Joy Borne, Tandem, Flower Power (groovy '60 and '70s clothes ideal for Ibiza's nightlife), Chapeau Ibiza (for delightful head apparel by Francesca Kirby, the only milliner on the island), Salambo (Cristina Buscetto leatherwear), Bianca (light and summery Ibizan-style clothes) and María M (for more great leatherwear).

You are probably a little poorer by now, and your shopping bags may be heavy.

If you have decided to stay and have dinner in **Sant Rafael** itself rather than return to Eivissa, I will wager that the disco sounds of **Privilege** or **Amnesia** – perhaps both – have lured you inside and you may want to keep the adrenalin pumping until the early morning. Still, it is my own suggestion that you turn in fairly early tonight save your energy for tomorrow's 'disco odyssey' which follows a lazy day on the beach.

Dinner on the terrace

DAY 4

Beach Day and Disco Odyssey

My suggestion is that you spend a very lazy day on a beach to recover from the past three days and get into shape for an all-night and wee-hours bash which takes in most of the top spots of Ibiza's exuberant nightlife. This strenuous, eye-boggling and ear-popping experience will be quite pricey. Entry, with one drink, to four discos is going to cost at least **12,000 pesetas** per person. (It will help if one of your party is a teetotaller, or volunteers to be for one night, and you can use your hire car rather than taxis.)

Some minor maintenance

Start off at **Marina Botafoch** at around 8pm. See the rich collection of yachts, motor cruisers and power boats. You may go green with envy. Stroll around to look at the boat showrooms and boutiques such as **Dora Herbst**. Then take a seat at **Madrigal** or **Mar y Sol II** cafés among the yachties, trendies and wannabes. There may even be live music at the latter. Stay at least until after what may be a beautiful sunset and the floodlights come on over Dalt Vila across the shimmering waters of the harbour. Then move on to **La Marina quarter**.

Here you will join a thronging crowd, ever-moving among gas-lit stalls selling local crafts and imported junk, packed streetside restaurant tables, busy bars and boutiques. Move with it, any way you like, through the cacophony of competing music. You will be gawped at and you can gawp back. Preening themselves will be the poseurs; wanting to look anonymous may be some famous faces; looking bemused will be shirtless youths in Union Jack shorts on an outing from Sant Antoni. There are better places to buy crafts (see *Pick & Mix* Options 1 and 2). Have a drink at one of the smart bars, such as **La Tierra** in Callejón Trinidad.

By now your stomach may be rumbling. On your passage through the alleys you may have seen a restaurant, among the many, that took your fancy. Try it, or go to one of the following long-time

Marina fashion show

Pre-disco crowd at Zoo Bar

survivors in a competitive scene where service is perfunctory and presentation is not highly imaginative. Still, they are lively and reasonably priced. **Restaurant Formentera**, in the old port, has tables both outside and inside and has a good selection of seafood dishes and more standard international fare (tel: 31 10 24). **El Delfin Verde** and **El Sausalito**, along the harbourside Calle Cipriano Garijo, are equally good and the last is my favourite of the two. As an alternative, there is the cheaper **Il Pavone**, Mayor 22 (tel: 31 35 55), with a tiny balcony and a terrace from which to watch the parade below.

After dinner, get some exercise by taking a stroll along the harbour wall. You will be rewarded by memorable views of Dalt Vila, hauntingly floodlit, and the bright lights of the town below. Then, you simply must go to **Zoo Bar** on the Plaza Antoni Riquer. Drinks are relatively expensive but the crowd here is a picture show worth the price. It is the pre-disco stomping ground where nightbirds display their feathers – and some of these fowl are very exotic. If your own plumage is sufficiently impressive, you may even be given a free pass to one or more of the top discos. After lingering over your drink, walk the short distance to see what live music is on at the **Pereira café-bar**, Calle Conde Rosellón. It might be good jazz, rock or blues.

It will be around 1am by now and time to head for **Pacha** on the other side of the harbour, the first stop on your disco odyssey. Perhaps, make a quick detour through the nearby **Keeper complex** of open-air bars where scenemakers gather. Pacha, one of a chain of some

20 discos, opened in 1973 and maintains its autonomy. It led the way in creating theme parties with such names as Spanish Night and Flower Power, still very successfully organised by the frenetic Francisco Ferrer. The club is laid out in a number of small seating or dancing areas on different levels and, although it has 15 bars and capacity for around 3,000 people, **Pacha** has an intimate atmosphere, much favoured by residents. At the other end of the scale **El Divino**, located in the Puerto Deportivo Nuevo (tel: 19 01 76) is a truly spectacular club on a grand scale. Its huge terrace juts out over the rocks and the sea, offering stunning views of Dalt Vila in the distance. The interior is based on a Buddhist temple, with antiques, Krishna paintings and other mystical scenes. People will still be arriving when you leave about 2.30am to make your way to Sant Rafael.

Privilege (formerly the famous KU) is vast, with a swimming pool and multi-coloured fountain. In efforts to maintain/regain its position as Ibiza's leading club, its owners make great efforts to attract top quality performers and DJs, including holding a 'Cream' night on Thursday, when top DJs are brought in from all over the word. There are numerous bars and some quiet spots, a boutique and fine restaurant serving Basque cuisine, and very efficient staff. A new area has been created in the disco and on Friday nights this *Zona de la Vaca* becomes a gay zone. It is probably not an exaggeration to say that people who like discos and have been to the world's best remain deprived if they have not experienced Privilege on a night when Brasilio, the artistic director, has it humming at its best.

At around 4.30am, the crowd will be starting to thin. Join those moving on to nearby **Amnesia**. White and green predominate in this converted old *finca* with its luxuriant, cleverly conceived garden,

Privilege gained a world-wide reputation as KU

The 'in' crowd at Pacha

now also glass-covered. Here too, is a disco with an intimate atmosphere, another special favourite of permanent residents and regular visitors to the island. Like the others, Amnesia also stages theme parties. But at this time of the morning you will be catching only the tail end of any such activity and will find yourself among predominantly young people with strong staying-power. Leave after about an hour. But do not give up and go home quite yet!

It is a short trip back to **Eivissa**, to the basic **Maravilla Bar** on Plaça Constitució. Have a reviving cup of coffee and a delicious ham and tomato sandwich as you watch working class Eivissa come to life and realise that hedonism needs the support of other people's work. Then move up to **Plaça Espanya** in **Dalt Vila** to see the sun rise over Punta Grossa. The *calles* of this ancient quarter will be deserted now, cool and especially evocative. A walk through them will make for a lasting memory.

'Phew! It is definitely time for bed,' you may be saying. Not so, if you want to be able to say you were a short-stay visitor who did it all. You still have to go to **Space**, the ultra-modern, barn-like disco in Platja d'en Bossa. And in the main dance hall the sound is very loud indeed. The crowd is likely to be young, and quite a few will be visibly fading by now. The beat will be incessant until around 10am, however. Your brain will probably want to check out before then.

Less than 15 minutes away to the south is **Las Salinas beach**. Go to the eastern end, strip and have a refreshing swim. Then laze and doze on the beach for as long as you wish while you get an all-over tan. There is a bar when your thirst and hunger need satisfying. As the morning wears on and more people arrive, you may recognise some of the night-owls encountered during the course of last night's odyssey. By now they will have shed their nocturnal feathers and some may look better for it. You yourself are entitled to don a smirk of success, however: you have done it all on Ibiza,

A good way to recover after a hard night's dancing

Ibiza by Powerboat

A day-long boat tour of Ibiza's coastline, with time out for bathing and a picnic lunch, starting out from Marina Botafoch.

It will help spread the cost of this outing if you can make up a party of five, preferably including someone who has a certificate of competence, that is a second-class skipper's ticket from his or her home country for boats of up to 8m (26ft). Otherwise, a party of four can hire a skipper at 15,000 pesetas for the day. The cost of a 175-horsepower boat will be around 53,000 pesetas during the peak months of July and August.

Most of the yacht hiring companies are at **Marina Botafoch**, on the wharf which separates the Botafoch and Eivissa Nova marinas. Also at Marina Botafoch and hiring speedboats are **Cruiser Ibiza** (tel: 31 40 10), **Marbella Charter** (tel: 31 40 10), **Keywest** (tel: 31

A Marina Botafoch bar: gathering place for would-be cruisers

60 70) and **Coral Yachting** (tel: 31 96 26). Sailboat fanatics can try **Moorings** in Santa Eulàlia (tel: 908 09 7354).

You may be tempted to try circumnavigating Ibiza in its entirety. Forget it. What follows is a suggestion for a more leisurely day, taking in beaches, islets and coves and allowing time for lots of swimming. Accept suggestions from the hire company or your

One of many calas

hired skipper, if you have one. Taking along a picnic lunch increases your freedom to do as you please. Some hotels will prepare one or you can make up your own (see the *Shopping* section for places to buy food and drink). Alternatively, there are *merenderos* or beach restaurants at many of the places you will be visiting.

Head south, going slowly to take in views of **Dalt Vila** and the protective cliffs on which it was built. Thrill to full power as you speed to **Es Cavallet**, Ibiza's official nudist beach. After a bare-bottomed swim here, if you like, move on past the Torre de ses Portes watchtower to the **islet of Espalmador**, which is a popular bathing spot for people with boats. Here and at your next stop, long, sandy **Platja de ses Illetes** on the northern strip of **Formentera**, you will be among the day's earliest arrivals.

A little further south, take a quick look at **Sa Savina**, Formentera's port village. Then it is full speed northwest to the tiny fishermen's bay of **Sa Caleta**, on Ibiza's south coast. Around the point is bigger **Cala Jondal**. Its pebbly beach is backed by a good bar-restaurant. Move on from here, hugging the coastal cliffs, along one of the most unspoilt areas of Ibizan coastline.

You may want to drop anchor again in **Cala d'es Cubells**. When swimming toward shore, mind the sea urchins on the rocks. You may see people picking them off to eat straight from the shell, but they are difficult to handle and definitely an acquired taste.

After the isolated *cala* (cove) and point of **Cabo Llentrisca**, approach the impressive rock of Es Vedra which rises to 382m (1,253ft). Circle it slowly and quietly to discover if it exudes any magical

Roaring past Dalt Vila

power for you: it does for some islanders. For them it is benevolently spooky and gives off good vibrations. Tales of Es Vedra include that of an exiled priest who lived solely off milk sucked directly from the udders of the wild goats which lived on these precipitous cliffs. The pinnacle is also claimed to be one of Hannibal's many birthplaces as well as an islet in Homer's *Odyssey* from which the Sirens called to Odysseus.

Nearby is the long sandy beach of **Cala d'Hort** and the more intimate **Cala Garbo**. Quite a few boats are likely to be at anchor in the very pretty **Cala Vedella**. Join them for a while. Depending on how long you have lingered at stops on your way here, you may or may not have time for a sprint northwards to get a view of the coves to which the excursion boats bring trippers from **Sant Antoni**, such as Cala Conta and Cala Bassa. Enter Sant Antoni's wide bay and scoot around the islet of Conillera. On the way back to

The bay at Sant Antoni

Eivissa, stop in at **Las Salinas beach** where there will still be a playful crowd of the 'beautiful people', their bodies even browner in the light of the setting sun. Then, power back to Marina Botafoch to arrive before 9pm.

Visitors for whom a full day at sea is likely to prove too long will find an assortment of shorter boat trips, some in glass-bottomed boats allowing glimpses of the marine life, and half-day excursions available. Eivissa (including Figueretes), Sant Antoni, Portinatx and Santa Eulàlia offer the most frequent departures, but check what particular tours are available during your visit. The following are just a few examples of the likely options.

On Sunday during July and August there is an early departure from **Santa Eulàlia** for a 9-hour boat trip around the island. From Santa Eulàlia there are also regular services to **Cala Llonga** and to the resort areas north. Less regularly there are boats to **Portinatx**. Combine this trip with one from Eivissa to Santa Eulàlia and you will cover most of the east coast. To view most of the largely untouched northwest coast you can take the 2-hour trip from **Sant Antoni** to Portinatx. On Tuesday, Thursday and Saturday in season boats depart at 10am and return at 5pm. From Sant Antoni there is a choice of trips linking the resorts along the southwest coast and some include a circuit of **Es Vedra**. Bon voyage!

PICK

1. Punta Arabi and Las Dalias Market

Wednesday morning or afternoon visit to Punta Arabi, including the 1960s-style market stalls manned by alternative lifestylers; plus Saturday afternoon at the Las Dalias market; lunch or dinner at Las Dalias Restaurant followed by live musical entertainment after dark.

From about 11am until late afternoon, coaches arrive at **Punta Arabi** to disgorge holidaymakers at what is one of the island's biggest attractions – among its few. Punta Arabi is essentially an attempted re-creation of Ibiza in the 1960s, when colourful people colonised Ibiza and scraped together a living selling arts and crafts and utility items which they made themselves. The burgeoning collection of stalls is itself very colourful and so are some of the stall-holders but, for the most part, I feel this is a weekly stage set-up

Ibiza's hippy markets are a feature of island life

Es Canar: for joggers...

on which people play out roles for an audience of holidaymakers. Cameras click, some of the goods and 'hippies' provoke giggles, there is much handling of what is on show and asking of prices. But I see few people dipping into their pockets for cash or walking back to their coaches with parcels. So I wonder how many of the stallholders make any sort of living from the market. Some, of course, have other outlets for their wares.

I suggest you spend more time here than is usually allocated by the coach excursions because there is an interesting array of stuff on offer. Time is needed to look carefully at things, to sort out the genuine island work from the imports; to talk to the stallholders. Chatting with some of these interesting characters might be the most memorable part of your visit here. Your opening question should always be, 'Were these things actually made by you yourself?' Buying something from someone who has shared with you a bit about his or her life and work on the island makes for a more satisfying memento of your visit. To get to Punta Arabi, go to **Es Canar**, to the right at the end of the small harbour and then follow signs to the **Hippy Market**.

...and potters

Yaron, making bongo drums at Las Dalias

After your time here you might take this opportunity to escape the crowds and see a bit more of the northern east coast. From Es Canar take a back road marked **Cala Llenya** which has a big sandy beach and offers good opportunities for watersports. (See also *Day 2, page 32.*)

On Saturday, another **hippy market** happens from around 11am–8pm on the left side of the road from Santa Eulàlia to **Sant Carles**, just before the entrance to the hamlet. It is, I think, better than Wednesday's Punta Arabi market; smaller but with a greater concentration of genuine craftwork. Here you can also buy inexpensive, unconventional clothing, both new and secondhand. Among the maze of stalls, you are sure to come across **Yaron**, who makes wind chimes and big bongo drums. If you happen to be in Las Dalias in June, you might catch a belly dancing show performed by Yaron's wife Nurbanu. Also look out for **Udo's** lathe creations. His pipes, board games, mazes and children's toys are all made from local wood. For an interesting range of leather goods, look around for **Dario Bomé**'s stall.

Las Dalias Restaurant is open for lunch and dinner. It is cool and spacious with beamed ceilings and old farming implements as decoration. The menu is international, and reasonably priced. The bar is almost always lively with a mix of unusual characters. Las Dalias is also one of the most active venues on the island for a variety of **live music**, usually advertised on posters around the island. You could come here at around 2–3pm, have lunch and then browse in the market. Or come in the late afternoon, see the market, spend some time in the bar, have a meal and then take in the live entertainment. (*See also Day 2, page 32.*)

Hotel Hacienda buffet

2. Hotel Hacienda Barbecue or Sunday Buffet

Thursday afternoon and evening in Port de Sant Miguel, including a drive through the countryside to Santa Agnés and Sant Mateu; plus a sumptuous barbecue at the Hotel Hacienda. Alternatively, gala Sunday buffet luncheon at the hotel, followed by a dip in the pool.

Before setting out, call to make a reservation for the evening barbecue at the Hotel Hacienda (tel: 33 30 46/33 45 00). Set out just after 4pm to drive from **Sant Rafael** to **Santa Agnés**. It is one of the prettiest drives on the island: first through open coun-

The pool, Hotel Hacienda

tryside, orange groves and vineyards, then between two hills thickly covered with pines. In Santa Agnés the bar-cafeteria **Can Cosmi** is known for its good *tortillas* (omelettes) which you may wish to sample if you are peckish. They will not mind if you share one. **Can Sabatier** is an *artesanía* in leather, well worth popping into if it is open. The road from here to Sant Mateu passes through the Corona valley, an area devoted to dry-farming where old-timers work the red soil using ancient methods. Here and on the road to Sant Miquel you traverse the best of Ibiza's biblically simple landscapes. If you want to photograph any of these traditional people and their homes, do them the courtesy of asking their kind permission beforehand.

Scheduled for 6.15pm on Thursday only (admission: 500 pesetas), but usually starting a little later, there is a performance of *bal pagés* (country dancing) in the courtyard of **Sant Miquel's church** which crowns the small hill above the village. Parking nearby can be difficult so allow a little time to find a space. These are dances about love, marriage and family which a *compère* explains in four languages before each set – a somewhat tiresome interruption of the festivities. The women's costumes are especially beautiful, complemented by shawls of gold thread and heavy jew-

Country dancing at Sant Miquel

Hacienda poultry display

ellery. The men, wearing red caps and cummerbunds, use locally made *castanyoles*, large castanets with a distinctive sound.

Take the road marked Port de Sant Miquel which snakes down through more of the island's enchantingly gentle scenery. At the start of the port resort's development go right at the sign for Coves de Ca Na Marça. I do not rate a visit to these **illuminated caves** particularly highly but, if you want to see them, conducted tours are available (the caves are open: 15 May to end October 10am–7pm; admission: 600 pesetas).

' The real purpose of coming on this road is to see **Port de Sant Miquel** from the heights. It is a prettier view from a distance and you may agree with me that it would have been better if building permission had not been given for some of the more recent structures raised here. Back down again, turn left and soon right on the small road signposted **Hotel Hacienda**, which twists up to the island's top hotel.

You should have called ahead to make a reservation for the Thursday night barbecue around the pool. This involves gourmet barbecueing of fine seafood and meats.

Alternatively, you might choose to set out on this trip earlier in the day and take advantage of the Hotel Hacienda's **Sunday buffet luncheon**. Phone ahead to reserve a table for the buffet at 1.30pm (tel: 33 45 00). After almost 30 years of worldwide travel, I still rate the presentation of the Hotel Hacienda's Sunday lunch among the most tempting and memorable displays of food I have seen anywhere. As the chef, insists, 'It is not only the presentation which must be brilliant, but the taste must be delectable.' It is. The hotel comprises a cluster of low whitewashed buildings whose design is inspired by Ibiza's traditional domestic architecture. Luncheon guests are seated at impeccably dressed tables on a covered terrace facing the big swimming pool. Beyond, cliffs plunge into the sea and above them is a vista of untouched pinewoods. This view will not change for the land's owners have foresworn selling any of it for development.

Including tax but excluding wines and other drinks, the cost of the buffet is around 6,400 pesetas per person – in my estimation, excellent value for money. The hotel is reached by turning left just before entering Port de Sant Miguel. Though the buffet lunch goes on for as long as you wish to stay, I suggest you get there around starting time. And take your bathing gear for a **swim** in the pool during the afternoon. Incidentally, on Friday evenings there is live music and on Saturdays a salsa band.

3. Ibiza on Foot

Walking in the vicinity of Sant Mateu, or in three specific areas located along the island's coast, introduces you to a more pastoral, unspoilt side of Ibiza.

Ibiza's large areas of flat terrain crossed by quiet minor roads, farm tracks and paths make for easy walking through the island's interior. There are many places where you can park your car and simply stroll for an hour or so, enabling you to see at first hand, pockets of Ibiza which remain untouched by the tourist boom. You are also likely to come across at least one *ca eivissenc*, or Ibizan hound, which, as all breeders will tell you, exhibits similarities to the ancient hounds of Egypt. Large paws and long legs support a lean body with tan and white markings; pointed ears above a long snout. Hunters of rabbits and hares like them for their lightness

The Platja d'en Bossa

and speed but the breed does not have a reputation for being especially brainy.

I do not like the idea of suggesting precisely mapped walking routes in the countryside so that the privacy of people living along these routes is threatened. One idea, however, is to park in the hamlet of **Sant Mateu** and set off on the gravel road leading north. A 3–4-hour stroll along what is a public road – you can take side tracks as you find them – will bring you back to Sant Mateu.

On an island there are obviously many enjoyable coastal walks. Suggestions for three easy ones are: bus or taxi from Eivissa to the end of **Platja d'en Bossa** and then a 3-hour walk to **Las Salinas beach** from which you take a bus back to Eivissa; from the yacht marina in **Santa Eulàlia**, a 2-hour walk to **Es Canar** and a bus or boat back to Santa Eulàlia; from **Sant Antoni** by bus or boat to **Cala Bassa** and then a 2½–3-hour walk to **Cala Codolar** from where you take a bus or boat back to Sant Antoni. You will have to check bus and boat timetables locally.

Do most of your walking before noon or in the late afternoon; dress lightly in summer and wear some headcover, as well as firm shoes with a good grip; do not forget your bathing gear and sun protection cream; take an adequate supply of water and something to nibble; basic first aid supplies of a disinfectant, plasters and a bandage or two would be a sensible addition to your knapsack. It is wise to walk with a companion and to tell somebody where you are going and when you expect to be back. I have not met any unchained, aggressive dogs on the island. And there is another walker's delight: Ibiza has no dangerous creepy-crawlies. If you come across any gates, you will, of course, close them behind you.

Boats for hire, Santa Eulàlia

4. Sport and Fitness at Ahmara

Pump iron, take an aerobics class, or lounge in the Turkish bath or Jacuzzi – and then repair the damage in the beauty salon at the Ahmara Sport and Social Centre.

The **Ahmara Sport and Social Centre** is still a modest establishment, as ambitious plans for refurbishment and expansion have not yet come to fruition. But probably because it is small and unpretentious, it scores for being friendly and having a family feel. It also remains the best place on the island for visitors seeking to engage in a variety of **sports**, work-out with supervision, enjoy a sauna and massage, and procure **beauty treatments**. Here you can exercise your

The island presents plenty of opportunities for outdoor recreation

competitive spirit as well as play a game of squash, badminton or tennis (there are four squash courts, two tennis courts and one badminton court). Take along a playing partner or arrange a game with someone else at the centre looking for an opponent. You can also get tuition in these sports. A series of competitions in different leagues are regularly run for members.

For aficionados, there is an array of Nautilus exercise machines in addition to exercise classes and a big, all-marble Turkish bath (like a *hammam*). At 37°C (98.6°F), the water of the communal jacuzzi brings instant relief to aching muscles. After a work-out, guests may opt for a soothing massage or a stretch working on their tans in the solarium. Outside, a large swimming pool is welcoming.

Other facilities include a beauty salon and hairdresser for which appointments should be made. The indoor/outdoor **restaurant** is open for lunch and dinner from Monday to Saturday (Sunday closed all day). Restaurant guests may use the pool. There are different price scales for use of the facilities by both members and non-members. In the summer of 1995 a full-day ticket costing 4,200 pesetas allowed use of all facilities.

The centre is open midday–midnight (information and reservations, tel: 39 69 45; fax: 39 01 69). It is located about 3km (1¼ miles) along on the Eivissa–Sant Josep road, well signposted on the left-hand side.

Nightlife

Many places compete with Ibiza's holiday offerings of sun, sea and sand but I do not know any other which can compete with the scintillating scenario which Ibiza's top impresarios of the night create. One of these men and the originator of the Pacha concept, Ricardo Urgel, claims, 'The international success of Ibiza is to a large extent due to its discos.' Ibiza had to come up with something extraordinary to amuse bright, easily bored people from the world's cities through its summer nights. I would guess that for the majority of its fashionable, highly solvent visitors the island's nightlife is at least half of its attraction.

Day 4 is my suggestion for a progression through much of Ibiza's night scene including the top discos of **Pacha**, **El Divino**, **Privilege** (formerly KU), **Amnesia** and **Space**. Remember that discos only begin to stir into life after 1am.

Ibiza's summer nights are legendary all over Europe

El Divino (admission: around 3,500 pesetas), in the Puerto Deportivo Nuevo in Eivissa, is the current favourite. Its oriental-style interior is filled with eastern antiques, Krishna paintings and mystic clouds floating across the walls. Its vast terrace juts out across the ocean and offers stunning views of the Dalt Vila. Theme nights are held on Wednesday and Saturday. Other special nights have included a 'Noche Flamenca', a 24 Juillet Party, a Hollywood night, a Flower Power night and a traditional Ibizan Full Moon Party. Both El Divino (tel: 19 01 76) and Pacha (tel: 31 36 12) have restaurants noted for their excellent Basque cuisine and atmosphere (best between midnight and 3am).

Privilege (admission between 4,000 and 6,000 pesetas), which as KU was for so long the top club in Ibiza, tries hard to regain its top-dog status. Rumours of its degeneration have prompted the new owners to make strenuous efforts to attract top-class perform-

Dressed up and ready to go

ers and DJs. It too has a first-rate restaurant. Other discos which try to emulate the top venues but where entrance charges are lower and the crowd is usually younger are: **Angel's** on Eivissa's Paseo Marítimo; **Xaloc** in Figueretes; **Kiss** in Platja d'en Bossa; and **Es Paradís** in Sant Antoni. **Lola's**, in Eivissa's Sa Penya, is intimate and exotic and the island's oldest disco.

A choice of music bars satisfies most tastes. The sound of music is never far away in the streets as it drifts out from bars: old familiars and the latest sounds often clashing irritatingly. The island authorities have been conducting a campaign against noise pollution which has been only partly successful. Look for handouts and posters which advertise live music events. The best places to find live music regularly are **Concierto Bar Pereira** in Eivissa (*see Day 4, page 40*) and **Las Dalias** in the countryside (*Pick & Mix Option 1, page 49*). There are also live concerts at Privilege (tel: 19 80 86) three or four times a year. Check trade publications and the local newspaper for information.

Of course, it is possible to experience the nightlife on Ibiza without going to any of the places I have singled out. Many visitors to the island do just that, making perhaps only one sortie to Pacha, Amnesia, El Divino or Privilege. Much of the island's high life centres on villas or private functions in restaurants and hotels. If you don't manage to wangle an invitation to any of these, why not make up your own party with new acquaintances? Or try my preferred option: having enjoyed a fine meal on a warm and starry night being alone with the person you most care for, order a cool *cava*, and put your feet up on a terrace above a calm sea glimmering in the moonlight.

Both at its most hectic and its most tranquil, Ibiza is where romantic notions come most easily to mind.

The Casino, open until 5am

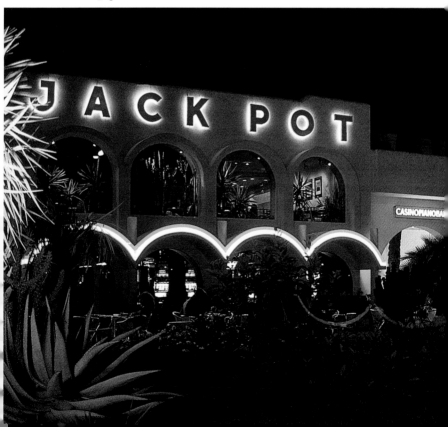

5. The Hippodrome and Casino

A flutter on the horses between dinner and disco at the Hipódromo Sant Rafael, or gaming at the Casino de Ibiza.

In July 1991, Ibiza gained a new nightlife venue when the **Hipódromo Sant Rafael**, situated on the Sant Rafael–Santa Eulàlia road, opened after major remodelling of the long-neglected horse racing track and the addition of a large viewing and entertainment complex. The idea was to create an entertainment which would fill the void between dinner and the time when the island's discos get into full swing at around 1am.

During the summer month evening races normally take place twice a week (Thursday and Saturday). Horses and riders, brightly coloured and active on the floodlit track, and the betting, are only part of the attraction here, though. The elegantly and exotically dressed spectators moving between the terrace bars in rhythm to the music pay more attention to one another than the racing and are equal partners in the night's action. Like other nightlife on Ibiza, nothing really gets going until fairly late, with the trotting races starting after midnight and going on until around 2.30am. Two television screens relay betting odds and results. The jockeys are local, and the horses French.

The vast number of betting windows in the betting hall makes laying bets and collecting winnings quick and easy. Minimum stakes are very low, so why not have a flutter?

The Hipódromo also provides Ibiza with a fine new venue for staging open-air events and extravaganzas. Be sure to check out what is on besides the racing during your stay.

If, like so many of the Spanish, you are an inveterate gambler, or if you are just a tentative novice in search of a fun experience while on holiday, you may want to move on to the **Casino de Ibiza** on Eivissa's Paseo Marítimo instead of a disco. The gaming room is open until 5am most nights during Ibiza's high season. Its fruit machine gallery and pizza parlour will also still be open at that very late, or alternatively early, hour.

While the rest of the island is partying, normal life must go on

6. Santa Eulàlia

An evening in Santa Eulàlia, dinner at Restaurante El Naranjo, and nightcap at the Miramar bar with dancing at Studio 64.

Santa Eulàlia is the island's tamest town, so go there for a change from Eivissa's thronging crowd. Reserve a table for dinner at **Restaurante El Naranjo** (Calle Sant Josep 31; tel: 33 03 24; closed Monday). Your evening visit may start up at **Puig d'en Missa** for your first, or yet another look, at the church, the old houses around it and the view from this high vantage point in the evening light. If the shops are still open, take a walk through the streets on the seaward side of the main road. Down the *rambla* there will be a string of stalls and usually one or two quick-portrait artists.

Church bell-tower

Take a walk along the **Paseo Marítimo** towards the marina for a look at the yachts and cruisers sheltering there. Then head back onto the main road (Sant Jaume) and to the main square for a drink at the **Royalty Bar**, the local equivalent for people-watching of Eivissa's Mar y Sol. Around the corner is Calle Sant Vicente which is lined with a selection of restaurants, many with outdoor tables. You may want to choose one of them if you were unable to book space at **Restaurante El Naranjo**. Here, indoors or on the orange-scented patio, Geoffrey Millburn and his partners have exhibited flair and take care in preparing and presenting dishes of local and French inspiration. The service is attentive and the quality-to-price ratio excellent.

After dinner, cross the main road and proceed into Calle Sant Joan where, at No 27, the **Miramar bar** is likely to have a crowd gathered for nightcaps or pre-disco juice. If moving to disco music or just watching others do so is what you want thereafter, nearby **Studio 64**, on the corner of Calle de Sant Llorenç, is Santa Eulàlia's top disco.

7. Shocking 'San An'

A night out on the town in notorious 'San An', or Sant Antoni, with its no-holds-barred nightlife and popular discos.

In contrast to comparatively staid Santa Eulàlia, **Sant Antoni** is the island's brash town. Come here to experience a night in an archetypal Mediterranean resort created by and for the budget end of Europe's package holiday industry and a local business community with little in mind but quick profits. You may find that the resort is not as dreadful as it has been painted in the sensationalist press of Britain, Germany and other countries. And, especially if you are youthful, your experience of San An may be highly enjoyable. Certainly, Sant Antoni's powers that be are set on a course to upgrade the town's tarnished image.

I leave you to your own devices to make what you will of San An and to find places to have an aperitif and meal. You may want to start off with a stroll along the waterfront **Paseo de ses Fonts** where the ferry and excursion boats are berthed. During the season there will be a string of 'craft' stalls and some quick-portrait artists. If you cross over near the bus station and into **Calle Ample**, there is a distinctive church in a part of town which still retains some vestiges of charm. Turn left, into the pedestrianised area of the 'West End', with **Calle Santa Agnés** at its centre. Here is San An at its liveliest and most garish. You may decide to leave and see if the less frenetic night scene on the south side of Sant Antoni is more to your taste. From the terrace of a beachside restaurant you can contemplate the bright town across the bay.

Sant Antoni has a wide array of music bars and discos to choose from. Beneath its pyramidal canopy, **Es Paradís** is considered the town's top venue. At nearby **Extasis**, another big disco, the younger tourist crowd is more exuberant.

Day-time excursions from Sant Antoni

8. Gay Ibiza Nights

Ibiza lives up to its reputation as a magnet for gay holidaymakers, as the catalogue of bars, restaurants and discos in Eivissa and Dalt Vila which cater for a predominantly gay clientele attest.

Places catering specifically to gay people tend to advertise each other: if you go into one there will be posters or cards to inform you about others. In Eivissa's **Sa Penya quarter** there is a concentration of gay bars at the seaward end of **Calle Virgen** (also known as Calle Mare de Deu) which start

filling with customers at around 10pm. They include: **Catwalk**, 42; **Galeria**, 64; **Bar JJ**, 79; and **Teatro**, 83. Some of the eating places in this street also have a largely gay clientele, including **Restaurante Sa Torre**, 78; **Foc i Fum**, 55, and **Rocky's**, 6.

Huddled below Dalt Vila's walls and with a large open terrace is **Incógnito**, Calle Santa Lucia, 21, a bar which gets busy later on in the evening. Nearby **Lola's**, Ibiza's oldest disco, has a sexually ambivalent atmosphere, and, also in this area, is the classic **Naranja Mecánica**. Along Alfonso XII you will find **El Dôme**, **Angelo**, and **L'Atrium**.

In **Dalt Vila** there are gay bars along **Sa Carrossa**. The terraces of **Restaurant Can den Parra**, Calle San Rafael, and **Restaurant La Scala**, Sa Carrossa, are popular dining spots. **La Muralla**, at the end of Sa Carrossa and looking up to Dalt Vila's walls, is a relaxing outdoor spot for an after-dinner drink. Around the corner, **Crisco** is a bar for leather-lovers. **Anfora**, Calle Sant Carles 5, is Ibiza's exclusively gay disco.

Discos like Pacha host gay nights

The colourful birds in its upstairs aviary often cannot compete with the gay plumage of some of its wingless customers. Spectacular drag queens under the artful direction of Phillip Michelle can be admired at **Sansara**. For lesbians, **Kinky Bar** on Calle Virgen (Calle Mare de Deu) and **Monroe's** in the Figueretes area are worth seeking out.

Gay people are not out of place at mainstream clubs such as **Privilege** or **Pacha** (*see page 41*), both of which regularly feature gay theme party nights. In addition, the former organises a gay night every Friday. Its 'Vaca Muerta' parties, with a round bed thrown in, are definitely worth experiencing.

9. A Day on Formentera

An excursion to nearby Formentera island by hydrofoil or ferry; exploration by hire car; lunch on Illetes beach followed by a swim; then back to Ibiza.

The day prior to this excursion, ask your car hire company if you can exchange your car on Ibiza for one on Formentera for one day. Make the necessary arrangements for leaving your Ibiza car, and its keys, at the rental firm's depot before 9am and collecting a car again before 9pm. If they will not cooperate in this way you will have to hire a car on arrival in **Sa Savina**.

You want to get the most out of a day on Formentera which means an early start. At 9am take the **Flebasa hydrofoil** from the quay diagonally opposite Café Mar y Sol. Buy a one-way ticket when you board; my suggestion is that you come back on the ferry boat. If you miss the hydrofoil, take the ferry boat or pricier rapid-jet of Trasmapi from the terminus (Estación Marítima) on the west side of the harbour. Buy a ticket inside the terminus building. Crossing times are, on average, 30 minutes for the hydrofoil and rapid-jet and an hour for the boat. Check the last departure times from Formentera but do not calculate on arriving just in time to

The best trips are boat trips

catch the last boat: it may be full.

Good views of Dalt Vila's profile above steep cliffs and then of Ibiza's southeastern coastline appear on the right. On the close approach to Formentera, the uninhabited island of **Espalmador**, which is a very popular destination for people with boats, appears on the left. Step ashore on the quay of Sa Savina's small port and it should not take more than a few minutes to collect the hire car from wher-

CARRER DE CARLES V
←
BC AUTOS IBIZA RENT A CAR S.A.
←

ever the Ibiza office directed you or to complete formalities for another hire. You will be thankful later if you now buy cold, bottled water and soft drinks from a shop or bar.

The idea is to make a quick orientation tour of this lambchop-shaped island followed by a leisurely seafood lunch and a long laze on a beach. That will give you an overall impression of Formentera, its low-key tourism offerings and laid-back lifestyle; enough, I think, to decide whether or not you would like to return for a longer visit. My bet is that you will want to return, if the simple pleasures of a sunshine beach holiday, as opposed to Ibiza's razzmatazz nightlife, are your priority.

First, a geography lesson is in order. Formentera consists of two high plateaux, Cap de Barbaria (102m/335ft) in the southeast, and La Mola (192m/630ft) in the west, linked by a thin and low-lying strip with Platja de Tramuntana along its northern edge and Platja de Migjorn along the south. Two lakes lie on either side of Sa Savina: Estany d'es Peix and Estany Pudent. North of the latter are the abandoned salt flats of Ses Salines, where developers with plans for tourist facilities were fortunately frustrated. A tiny digit of land points north to the islet of Espalmador: Platja de ses

Formentera fisherman prepares for his day

Illetes on its west and Platja de Llevant on the other side are, I think, the best beaches on either of the *Pitiüses*, or Pine Islands. Since the Greeks named these islands, Formentera has been much denuded of pine trees but they still grow in small clumps; junipers, carobs and spreading figs are also prevalent. Tempted by the easy profits to be made from land sales and work in the tourism industry, fewer and fewer families now continue the hard work of scraping a living from dry-farming, and many small fields now lie abandoned behind collapsing stone walls.

From Sa Savina it is only 3km (1¾ miles) to **Sant Francesc**, the island's 'capital'. Its size and pace immediately indicate that Ibiza and Formentera are worlds apart in every sense but the geographical. After a walk around its few streets, set

Cliffs by La Mola

Lighthouse at La Mola

off south to **Cala Saona**, a small sandy bay surrounded by cliffs and pine copses where small-scale tourism development has not been obtrusive. From here you may want to go down to the desolate end of **Cap de Barbaria**.

Back to Sant Francesc and on to Sant Ferran which you bypass for now as you amble along the straight road of the island's central strip. After Es Caló the road rises among pines and there is a mirador at which to stop and take in a view of the island. Further on is the hamlet of **El Pilar** with its distinctive church and a few places selling craft products. Make sure to visit the ceramicists, and the *mercería* next to Bar El Pilar which sells woollen articles. Ahead, **La Mola lighthouse** sits high above sheer cliffs. Backtrack to just past the *mirador* and turn left to the resort complexes of Club La Mola and Mar y Land. If you think it is time for a swim and you do not want to join the crowds on the beach, walk a little to the east and find seclusion among the rocks. Return to the 'main' road and go right into **Es Caló**, a tiny port in use since Roman times. Then continue towards Sant Ferran but turn right at the sign to Es Ca Marí/Platja Migjorn to reach another, but more modest, area of holiday accommodation. In **Sant Ferran** enquire about the way to the **Fonda Pepe**, an institution on the island, which alternative lifestylers of the 1960s made their own and where a mixed bag of island characters and visitors still gather today. The heady, herby aroma of marijuana smoke may assail your nostrils while you have a drink here.

On to **Es Pujols**, the island's resort town. Have a quick look around and you will probably think how wonderful it would be if the Mediterranean was blessed with more resort developments such as this along its shores rather than the many concrete bunkers

Try the seafood at Es Molí

which the package holiday industry has spawned. It will be after 2pm by now and your quest is to get a table at **Restaurante Es Molí de Sal** (tel: 908 136773), which is near the start of **Illetes beach**. If you cannot find a table now, immediately book one for later and in the meantime enjoy the beach. At Es Molí the choice is of **seafood**, cooking is good and simple, service is professional and the site is superb. If you can, choose the locally caught *langosta*; islanders claim it is the Mediterranean's tastiest; I think it is delectable. The chilled white wine you have probably had will make sure there is no alternative but to spend the rest of the afternoon on the beach. Strip totally if you like: there are few places on Formentera where nudism raises eyebrows and this is certainly not one. My guess is that, after today's excellent outing, you will be most unwilling to head back to Sa Savina to catch the ferry to Ibiza! If so, see below.

Time to hire a bicycle

10. Two Days on Formentera

For details on getting to Formentera, consult 'A Day on Formentera' (page 64), but forget about car hire.

My suggestion for this two-day excursion to Ibiza's peaceful neighbour uses a more environmentally friendly means of getting about – either by bicycle, horseback or on foot.

I would play it safe and reserve accommodation in advance, preferably choosing a *hostal* room in **Es Pujols**, which is within easy walking or riding distance of the best beaches and Formentera's most

Nude sunbathing is particularly popular on Formentera

interesting hamlet, Sant Ferran. Es Pujols is also the liveliest place to be at night. My favourite place to stay here is the **Hostal Voramar** (tel: 32 81 19), but other options worth considering are **Sa Volta, Levante** and **Tahiti**. Bookings for these and other *hostals* can be made through **Viajes Islamar**, Calle d'Espalmador, Es Pujols (tel: 32 82 79).

To venture down the coast, perhaps to find a secluded spot for bathing, you can rent a rowing boat or dinghy, or even a windsurfer, if you like. Alternatively, explore the interior by hiring a bicycle or horse. There are a number of places in Sa Savina and Es Pujols where you can hire a **bicycle**. Contact **Alquiler Bicicletas** ETLS, Edificio Almadraba, Sa Savina (tel: 32 22 75) if you want to phone ahead and discuss your needs and be sure of getting what you want. Bicycles can also be hired in the port. To find out about both bike hire and horse riding, contact the **Formentera Tourist Office**, tel: 32 20 57.

With regard to **walking** on Formentera, you need little in the way of preparation (other than a supply of drinking water) and there can be few places where it is more enjoyable: just be sensible about not doing too much during the day's hottest hours and be sure to cover your head and neck. Exploring idyllic Formentera in this way will not only be a pleasure but also a priceless reminder in the simple pleasures you can still enjoy in our fast-paced world – if you take the time.

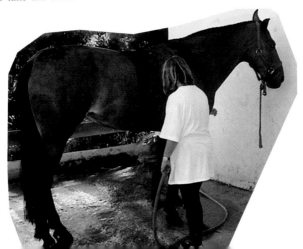

Shopping

As on most islands, imported commodities are likely to be more expensive. Another factor which tends to push up prices is that shopkeepers dependent on tourists have a relatively short season in which to make their profits. Many close down altogether in the off-season. Shopping on Ibiza is such a pleasurable pastime, however, and almost essential for the full enjoyment of your stay, that sometimes paying more for purchases than you would elsewhere becomes less of a consideration. Ibiza and Formentera have a high concentration of artists and artisans, and it is their creations which are the best buys: art, crafts, clothing and fashion accessories.

Where to Shop

In **Eivissa** the prime shopping area is along the streets and alleys of La Marina and lower parts of Sa Penya, the area of the Eixample on either side of Paseo Vara del Rey and Plaça de la Vila in Dalt Vila. **Sant Antoni** and **Santa Eulàlia** also have some good

Good place for a hat

shops among concentrations of places selling tourist tat. **Santa Gertrudis, Sant Josep** and **Sant Miquel** each have a few places worth looking into. **Sant Rafael** has a number of *cerámicas*.

Shopping Hours

Generally, stores are open Monday to Saturday, from around 9.30am–1.30pm and 5–9pm but, like much else on the island, opening hours are flexible. During high season, the shops of La Marina and Sa Penya and in Dalt Vila tend to open later in the morning and reopen from around 7–11pm, or midnight; some may only open in the evening, Sunday is a normal shopping day.

What to Buy
Antiques and Bric-a-brac

Three places you may want to snoop around to find something you have always wanted or never knew you needed are: **Pan y Tomate**, Calle Montgrí in Eivissa, which sells rustic home decorations; **Casi Todo**, in Santa Gertrudis; **Timor**, Carretera Eivissa–Santa Eulàlia near the junction with the Portinatx road; and **El Palio** in Sant Josep. Other possibilities worth trying in Santa Gertrudis are **Punta A** and **Can Daifa** (Plaça de la Iglesia), as is **Galería Es Moli**, Carretera San Miguel, km 1.3 Santa Gertrudis.

Art

There is not enough space in any guidebook to single out and re-view the work of all of Ibiza's resident artists. If you want information about who does what and who, among the island's emerging, still unknown talents is worth buying now, before they become fa-

Contemporary art on display

mous, a chat with people who run art galleries and exhibition centres, such as **Kati Verdera,** of Galeria Carl van der Voort, and **Cati Costa** of Sa Nostra, will be instructive. Ibiza's art galleries exhibit not only the work of island artists but also feature some of the leading lights in Spain's contemporary art scene. The young Mallorcan-born **Miguel Barceló** is one of the hottest properties around.

There are numerous galleries of varying importance on Ibiza, and a few on Formentera. Among the best are: **Galeria Carl van der Voort**, Plaça de la Vila, 13, Dalt Vila (tel: 30 06 49); **Sa Nostra**, a cultural centre, Calle Aragón 11; **Es Moli**, Carretera Eivissa–Sant Miguel, km 1.3 Santa Gertrudis; **Galería Marta Torres**, Calle Conde Rossellón, Eivissa; **Galería Berri**, San Agustín, Carretera Sant Josep–Sant Antoni; **Galería Al-hadros**, Calle Aragón, 49, Eivissa; **Libro Azul**, a book shop-cum-art gallery in Santa

Gertrudis; and **Micus**, Nuestra Señora de Jesús, Eivissa, a painter's studio. There may also be exhibitions at the **Hotel Hacienda**, and the **casino**.

Crafts

The best market for genuine local crafts is at **Las Dalias** on Saturday, 11am–8pm (see *Option 1, page 48*). At **Punta Arabí's 'hippy market'** on Wednesday (*Pick & Mix Option 1, page 46*), there are also local crafts on some stalls among the many which carry imported stuff. The same applies to the array of stalls which are set up each night (from 8pm) in Eivissa's **La Marina quarter**, along **Sant Antoni's harbourfront** and on **Santa Eulàlia's** *paseo*. There is also a new craft market, **Sa'Casilla** (Sunday 4–10pm in summer), at km 11.4 on the Sant Antoni–Eivissa road.

Ceramics top the crafts list and there are many different sorts of utilitarian and decorative pieces, both traditional and more modern and imaginative designs. They may be roughly finished or finely formed, unglazed or glazed, plain, painted or tinted, sometimes including the use of decorative metals. I single out the work of three craftsmen in San Rafael: **Julio Bauza** (Es Moli, tel: 19 81 36), **Carlos Icardi** (Can Ferreret, tel: 19 81 06), and **Kinoto** (Can Kinoto, tel: 19 82 62), although my favourite is Bauza. For the long lasting pleasure their pieces will give, these craftsmen's prices are very reasonable.

Boutiques in Sa Penya

In addition to these **Cerámica Ca'n Negre**, Puig d'en Valls (left about 2km/1¼ miles off Carretera Eivissa–Sant Antoni), **Toni Frigola** can be seen turning out 'popular' pottery.

Jewellery is made by quite a number of foreigners resident on the island. Notable among the good work is that of **Gianni Rainaldi** of Sant Llorenç (tel: 908 839454).

Basketware, and other woven grass items such as table mats and straw hats, is simple and inexpensive. **José Pascual**, on Calle de la Creu, and **Mar y Costa**, on Calle Guillem de Montgrí, in Eivissa's La Marina, are two places with a good selection.

Interesting **wrought iron work** is done at the forge of **Can Vicenç Musson** in Sant Llorenç.

Other craft items to look for include **leather goods**, **knitwear** from Formentera, **embroidery** and articles of clothing made from **handpainted fabrics**.

Ad Lib

Smilya Mihailovitch, a princess in Ibizan high society, was the tireless promoter of the classic Ibizan fashion style known as Ad Lib, which for over 20 years not only dominated the fashion scene in Ibiza but also made a significant impact on the world's catwalks, influencing many top designers. Essentially, the clothing is white, denoting its origin on *La Isla Blanca*, and made from finely embroidered, lace and cotton materials. Contrasting colours are usually used sparingly to increase the visual impact of garments. Designers aim for something full, light and romantic, yet practical and comfortable, which allows women to express their own individual taste. Smilya, now dead, used to say Ad Lib grew out of the island's free spirit in the 1970s, its cosmopolitan creativity and women's wish to break free from the dictates of the couturiers of Paris, Rome and London.

Clothing and Accessories

Clothing is big business on Ibiza, and there are myriad small and intriguing speciality shops in which to look for fashions. My advice is to opt for locally designed wear and the island's own **Ad Lib** creations, as well as designer labels from the impressive crop of very talented designers who have flowered in recent years, putting Spain in the limelight of the fashion world. Look for creations by **Adolfo Domínguez, Sybilla**, and **José Tomas**.

The following list is a representative selection of shops in Eivissa's La Marina, Sa Penya and Dalt Vila quarters, and gives an idea of the choice available. Specific shops are also mentioned in the individual itineraries and *Pick & Mix* options.

Joy Borne's creative fashions

JOY BORNE
Calle Josep Verdera
This shop specialises in highly individual women's fashion in viscose. Good for special occasions.

TANDEM
Start of Calle Mare de Deu
A good range of leather fashions for both sexes. The clothes are designed on Ibiza but made in factories on the mainland.

SALAMBO
Calle José Verdera, 4
Tel: 31 16 19
Leather designs (up to size 42) by designer Cristina Buscetto, who heads a group of 10 designers committed to promoting Ibizan design at national and international levels.

MANA
Plaça de la Vila
Cotton clothes by Mana Llobet.

MARIA M
Calle Riambau, 2
Leather fashions for slim women.

Modelling fashion at Paula's

CHAPEAU IBIZA
Cale Montgrí, 12
Wonderful hats in straw, velvet, linen, etc, by milliner Francesca Kirby. Come here for all manner of headwear, from a simple sun visor to an elaborate wedding hat.

JESS I JOY
Calle La Cruz, 18
Trendy clothes for the younger crowd. Lycra, cotton and some leather fashion. Look out for Elisa F's popular lycra line.

BIANCA
Calle de la Virgen, 37
Ad Lib, Ibiza-style clothes (*see page 73*), summery and light.

PEPA BOTETT
Calle de la Cruz, 4
Good range of women's clothing and swimwear.

FLOWER POWER
Calle Montgrí
Groovy '60s and '70s clothing. Ideal for nightclub wear.

CHALECO IBIZA
Calle Montgrí
Handmade vests and handpainted silk ties are sold in this delightful, minuscule shop.

MONTGRISIMO
Calle Montgrí
This is essentially a gift shop, but it also sells an exciting range of costume jewellery ideal for glittering Ibizan nights.

FANNY FOX
Corner of Calles Peraires and Obrador
Flamenco dresses (something in which to startle friends at home, perhaps); cotton skirts and pretty handmade blouses.

VICTOR
Calle d'Enmig.
A wide selection of white cotton shirts in smart and comfortable designs, comparatively well-priced.

CAMPOS DE IBIZA
Calle Bisbe Azara.
Wonderful perfumes, luxury soaps and other toiletries to remind you of the island. Also bathrobes, towels and leisurewear.

CANTONADA
Calle Comte de Rosselló 10.

S'ESPADENYA
Calle Ignasi Riquer, Dalt Vila.
Espadrilles or *simples*, rope-soled shoes in a variety of designs and colours.

The choice of boutiques seems endless

Food and Drink

Meat, fish, charcuterie, vegetables and fruit: mornings, daily except Sunday and holidays in Eivissa's big *mercado*, off *calles* Catalunya and Extremadura, and in the markets of Sant Antoni and Santa Eulália. Fruit, vegetables and fish in the two small markets below the Portal de ses Taulas in Eivissa. Two good high-class grocery stores are: the German charcuterie **Quefa**, Calle M Caietá Soler 6, Eivissa; **Casa Alfonso**, Calle Sant Vicent, Sant Antoni. Fresh and packaged foods, charcuterie, bakery, wines and liquors: **Hiper Centro**, Puig d'en Valls, Carretera Eivissa–Sant Antoni. Health foods: **Natural**, Calle M Caietá Soler 8; and **The Herb Shop**, Calle Sta Cruz, which has a wonderful array of natural and holistic remedies.

Food is available everywhere

Eating and drinking establishments on Ibiza reflect both the needs of the island's permanent and transient populations. Basic bars and eateries serve Ibizans with lower priced drinks and local dishes. The dining rooms of 'package' hotels and a plethora of cafeterias and restaurants of every description dish up stomach-fillers for budget holidaymakers who like to do their drinking in 'typical' bars, pubs and 'bierkellers'. More discriminating palates are satisfied in rustic or elegant restaurants where refined cooking of local and international dishes is offered. And there are some select drinking places where the music and clientele are quiet.

To dine very well you must put aside the notion that Spain is cheap. Just as elsewhere, fine cuisine and high standards of service mean having to pay higher prices. But nobody used to dining in the top restaurants of London, Berlin or New York could possibly consider Ibiza's best to be expensive. And remember, some of your most lasting dining memories may be made over the simplest, most inexpensive meal at an unpretentious place where good-quality ingredients are plainly prepared. So much depends on the company with you at the table. Or think of summer evenings spent on a secluded beach with the person you love, grilling fresh fish and sipping cool wine beneath clear and starry Ibizan skies. Much of what makes eating out on Ibiza most memorable costs absolutely nothing.

Local Specialities

The Pine Islands have their own specialities, mainly peasant dishes making the best of local dry-farming produce, homegrown vegetables, fowl and small game, wild herbs and the harvest of the sea. Ibizans have adopted dishes from the other Balearic Islands, as they have from other regions of Spain, especially Catalonia. Within Spain the cooking of the Basque region and of Catalonia is the most highly rated.

On Ibiza the popular *sopas mallorquinas* of seasoned vegetables and bread have eggs added and the island's own *sopa de menuts* is made of chicken stock. *Sopa de rap*, a soup based on *rape* (monkfish) is also deliciously wholesome. *Arróssec* is the local form of rice-based *paella* with rabbit added to the chicken, mussels, prawns and a variety of vegetables. *Truita pagesa* is an omelette with potato, tomato and red pepper. Vegetarians should like *olla fresca*, a mix of various beans, potatoes and pears. For a snack, there are *cocas*, small pizzas with a topping of vegetables, fish or something sweet.

An international spread

Guisat de peix, a stew of fish, onion, tomato, potato, parsley, saffron, cinnamon, garlic and olive oil, is served as two dishes: the stew and then a plate of rice and cuttlefish which has been cooked in the stew stock. *Guisat de marisc* is a delicious shellfish stew. Other fish specialities not to be missed are: *burrida de rat-jada*, skate with a sauce of almond and crushed biscuit; *tonyina al'eivissenca*, tuna with pine nuts, eggs, lemon juice and dry white wine. The *langostas* (spiny lobsters) caught in local waters are delectable and so is *rotxa*, an odd-looking red fish of which the cheeks are the most prized part.

Sobrassades, red, spicy pork sausages, and *botifarrons*, blood sausage, are eaten by themselves as well as used in recipes. *Sofrit pages*, a peasant stew similar to many found elsewhere in the world, is the staple meat dish, incorporating local sausages, pork fat, chicken and lamb stock, potatoes and vegetables, seasoned and well cooked until the stock is much reduced. *Frita pagesa* is a fry-up of bits of pork meat and liver with red peppers, mushrooms and garlic, which is served with fried potatoes.

For feast days and holidays, *lechona asada*, roast suckling pig stuffed with herbs, is the usual favourite.

Among dishes featuring game and fowl are: *conill amb pebrots vermells*, rabbit with red peppers; and *perdíus amb col*, partridge with cabbage. Available in autumn and winter are *caragols cuinats*, snails in a thick stock of pork fat, local sausages and aromatic herbs. *En-*

Presentation at its best at Hotel Hacienda

saimadas, light pastries, often filled with cream, almond paste or a preserve, are eaten for breakfast or as a dessert. *Greixonera* is made with *ensaimada* or biscuit and flavoured with cinnamon and lemon. *Orietes* are aniseed flavoured cakes. And there is the ancient Carthaginian pudding called *flaó*, a cheesecake flavoured with mint (*see below*).

Punic Cuisine

One of the interests of Ernesto Ramón Fajarnés, Director of the Hotel Hacienda (tel: 33 30 46/33 45 00), is the cuisine of the Carthaginian period in Ibiza's history. You can sample his faithful recreations of some of this ancient people's dishes. Among the specialities frequently featured on the menu are asparagus with almond sauce; swordfish with *garum*, the favourite fish paste of both the Carthaginians and Romans; partridge with dates; pigeon with figs; and *flaó* (*see above*).

Drinks

Spain is a major producer of wines. Most of its best table wines, both red and white, come from the *Denominaciones de Origen* (controlled wine-growing areas) of Rioja and Penedés and you are safest in selecting from among these if you are not a Spanish wine buff. From Vega-Sicilia in the *DO* area of Ribero del Duero come Spain's most prestigious and priciest wines. Many *vinos de la casa* (house wines) offered in restaurants come from the Valdepeñas *DO*, a bulk producer of wines whose quality varies greatly. *Vi de taula pagés* is island wine, usually red or rosé with lots of body and plenty of kick. The Penedés area of Catalunya also produces *cava*, sparkling wines made by the champagne method, which are very good value and outsell French champagne in the US. With prices so low and quality so high, it is always a pleasure to pop the cork.

Coffee comes in many different styles but foreigners usually go for *café con leche* (with milk) or *café solo* (black). Tea is usually served with lemon. *Granizados* are freshly made fruit juices served with crushed ice. Often shockingly potent is *sangría*, a mix of red wine, brandy, fruits and juices, soda water and ice. Spanish *cervezas* (beers) are relatively strong at between 4.6–5.4 per cent alcohol by volume and many imported beers are available. Ask for almost any other alcoholic drink and you are sure to be able to get it, in measures larger than you are used to. Spain produces some fine *reserva coñacs* (brandies) and a great variety of liqueurs, of which many are *anís*, dry or sweet. As for water, stick with bottled *agua mineral*.

Some of the best cuisine is made from locally-gathered ingredients

Home from home

Herbes or *hierbas* are the island's herb-flavoured *anís* liqueurs of varying tastes and quality depending on what herbs have been used and which home recipe has been followed. They are either sweet or dry. Best known of the island's liqueurs and made in the Mari Mayans distillery are *frigola*, the local word for thyme, and *palo*, which is based on carob fruit. A small shop on the corner of *calles* Bisbe Torres and Bisbe Cardona in Eivissa's La Marina district has a good selection.

Meals and Dining Times

Hotels may offer a cooked breakfast (*desayuno*) but normally it is no more than coffee, tea or hot chocolate with pastries, breads or toast with jam or honey. There are places serving 'English Breakfasts'. For local people lunch (*la comida*) is the day's main meal and is taken after 2pm. Dinner (*cena*), a lighter meal at home, is eaten around 10pm and this is the best time to start thinking about sitting down in restaurants.

Recommendations

Recommendations have been made in the Day Itineraries and some *Pick & Mix* options and include the following places which you should not miss if you want to sample a wide range of the best Ibiza has to offer: **Celler Balear** and **S'Oficina** in Eivissa (Day 1); **Cala Mastella**'s *merendero* (also known as Chiringuito de Bigotes) (Day 2); **Lur Berri** in Sant Rafael (Day 3); **Hotel Hacienda** near Port de Sant Miquel (*Pick & Mix* Option 2); **El Naranjo** (*Pick &*

Cala Mastella's beach restaurant or 'merendero'

Mix, Option 6) **Molí de Sal** on Formentera (*Excursions*). Add to those the restaurants of **Pacha** and **El Divino** (see Day 4 and *Nightlife*) and **Les Jardins de Palerm** and **Pike's** (see hotels in *Practical Information*). A few more restaurants are included among my favourites, as much for the food as the location and ambience. That is not to say there are not others you will discover which merit equal recommendation. Always check opening times and make reservations.

EL CORSARIO
Calle Poniente 5, Dalt Vila
Tel: 30 12 48
Nothing fancy, but good and moderately priced. The terrace view is spectacular. Dinner only, closed Sunday.

CAN DEN PARRA
Calle Sant Rafael, Dalt Vila
Tel: 39 11 14
Inventive cooking for a lively cosmopolitan clientele.

LA PLAÇA
Plaça de Vila, Dalt Vila
Watch the *paseo* as you choose from a limited but carefully constructed selection. Reasonable prices.

CANA PEPETA
Carretera Eivissa–Portinatx km 15.4
Tel: 33 33 77
Housed in a traditional building with a shady terrace where Ibizan dishes of

chef Toni Tur ('Magret') can be enjoyed at fair prices. Closed Tuesday.

CANA JOANA
Carretera Eivissa/Sant Josep km 10
Tel: 80 01 58
Well-prepared local and international dishes with a touch of Catalan and Mediterranean influences. Terrace.

LA CASITA
Valverde, off Carretera Cala Llonga/
Santa Eulàlia
Tel: 33 02 93
Austrian staples plus innovative dishes. A thatched bar looks over a terrace surrounded by pines and oleander.

CANA ALFREDO
Paseo Vara de Rey, 16
Tel: 31 12 74
Family-run, with regional specialities. Good rice dishes and fish suquets. Reasonable prices.

CA'N DOMINGO DE CA'N BOTJA
Carretera Eivissa–Sant Josep, km 9.8
Restored masía-country house serving top quality Mediterranean cuisine.

DOÑA MARGARITA
Paseo Maritimo
Santa Eulàlia
Delicious seafood and great views of the marina and Formentera.

LAS DOS LUNAS
Carretera de Sant Antoni, km5.4
Tel: 19 81 02
Celebrity hang-out. Romantic garden, soft music, so-so Italian food.

Calendar of Special Events

The Pine Islands do not have the sort of spectacular *fiestas* and *ferias* which are celebrated at many places in mainland Spain. However, their festivities are still an opportunity for visitors to watch or join islanders in religious observances, and have fun. Each of the towns and hamlets has its *fiesta patronal* or patron saint's feast day, usually preceded by a *verbena*, a night of music and merrymaking.

These are times to see traditional dances and hear some of the older islanders, dressed in traditional costume, give renderings of songs which they alone keep alive. A *fiesta patronal* takes place somewhere on the islands every month of the year.

July and August are the months when most concerts of classical, jazz and pop music are scheduled at venues such as the cloister of the Ayuntamiento, the Iglesia de Santo Domingo and on the Baluarte de Santa Llúcia in Dalt Vila. Spanish and international pop stars give concerts at KU throughout the summer season. *Ibiza Jove* is a rock music festival held at the Hipódromo at the beginning of August. An international folklore festival is held in Sant Antoni near the end of August.

JANUARY

Fiesta patronal (Patron Saint) (17) in Sant Antoni.

FEBRUARY

Carnaval, banned by Franco, has been revived as a pre-Lent burst of indulgence and is celebrated through the month in Eivissa. On the 12th Santa Eulàlia celebrates its *fiesta patronal*.

MARCH / APRIL

Semana Santa (Easter Week): The procession in Eivissa on the night of Good Friday is the most impressive.

MAY

First Sunday: Santa Eulàlia celebrates with processions of decorated wagons and sports competitions.

JUNE

Fuegos de San Juan (24): bonfires and an impressive firework display illuminate Eivissa and its bay.

JULY

La Virgen del Carmen (16): maritime procession in Eivissa harbour in honour of the Patroness of sailors. There are similar celebrations in Sa Savina and Es Pujols on Formentera.

AUGUST

On the 5 August is the *fiesta* of the Patroness of Ibiza and Formentera, Nuestra Señora de las Nieves (Our Lady of the Snows – odd for a place which does not get snow). On 6 August *los Corsarios*, Ibiza's privateers, are honoured by celebrations in Eivissa harbour. On 8 August the Christian Reconquest is commemorated and it is the *fiesta* of San Ciriaco, Eivissa's patron saint. Celebrations end with another display of fireworks.

DECEMBER

Fiesta Patronal (3): in Sant Francesc Xavier, 'capital' of Formentera.

Public Holidays

In addition to local *fiesta* days and the changing dates for Easter and Whitsun, these are public holidays:

1 January	Año Nuevo
6 January	Día de los Reyes
19 March	San José
1 May	Día del Trabajo
24 June	San Juan
25 July	Santiago (Spain's Patron Saint)
15 August	Asunción
12 October	Hispanidad
1 November	Todos los Santos
8 December	Immaculada Concepción
25 December	Navidad

Traditional dancing

Practical Information

Orientation

Ibiza lies some 80km (49¾ miles) off mainland Spain's eastern Mediterranean coast. It and Formentera, together known as the Pine Islands, form a separate archipelago to that of larger Mallorca and Menorca to the north. The four islands constitute the *Comunitat Autonoma de les Illes Balears*, which is one of Spain's 17 Autonomous Communities and of which Palma de Mallorca is the capital.

Within the jurisdiction of the regional government, *Gobern Balear*, Ibiza and Formentera have their local council, *Consell Insular*, and a number of municipal authorities, *Ayuntamientos*. Ibiza's land area of 570km² (220 square miles) supports 80,000 people of whom 30,000 live in Eivissa, actually given the title of city by King Carlos III in the 18th century.

Eight thousand residents share Formentera's 80km² (31 square miles). Ferry trips from Eivissa to Sa Savina, Formentera's port, take about an hour by boat and 20 minutes by hydrofoil. In time, as in the main political issues, Spain is in line with the majority of EU countries: in summer two hours ahead of GMT; in winter one hour ahead. There has been a revival in the more widespread use of *Ibicenco* or *Eivissenc*, a dialect of Catalan, the Romance language which grew out of Provençal from the 7th century on and which is now spoken by around seven million people.

Most islanders also speak Castilian, the standard Spanish language. If you do not speak it, buy one of many good phrase books available. The telephone code for the Balearics is 971. Drop the 9 when dialling from abroad and first add 34, the code for Spain.

Climate and Clothing

The climate is typically Mediterranean which means hot summers, most rainfall during late autumn and the early part of relatively mild winters, and equitable and agreeable spring and autumn weather. Summer temperatures rarely exceed 40°C (104°F) or fall below 6°C (43°F) on the coldest winter night. There is something distinctly African as opposed to European about Ibiza and Formentera and the islands are open to climatic influences from that continent. The hilly area in the north of Ibiza, Els Amunts, rises no higher than 410m (1,345ft) at Puig Fornás but helps protect the island from the worst of Europe's winter influences. Although most rainfall usually occurs between October and December, I have in July experienced heavy thunderstorms which had the drain-covers dancing in Eivissa's streets.

Loose fitting cotton clothing is the obvious choice for summer; add some light sweaters for spring and autumn; things a little heavier and a light raincoat and umbrella for winter. Ibiza is a highly fashion conscious place. 'Anything goes' provided it is not kitsch. My advice is to arrive with a full wallet and a half empty suitcase and then to go shopping for locally designed clothing and accessories.

When to Go

The main season for visitors, when most places servicing them are functioning and Ibiza's wonderful nightlife is in full swing, is from mid-June to the end of September. If you want the islands to yourself, however, come outside these months, possibly in mid- to late spring.

How to Get There

Flying from international or Spanish departure points to Ibiza's airport using scheduled or charter services, with or without an accommodation 'package', is the preferred way to reach the island. It has been a complaint of islanders that their needs have been neglected by Iberia, Spain's national airline, and its subsidiary, Aviaco. Palma de Mallorca is much better serviced by regular and charter flights. The service from there to Ibiza is an up and down hop of 20 minutes.

New daily connections with Valencia and Alicante by Aviaco and Air Nostrum's propeller planes have been a great success. Other regular domestic connections are with Barcelona, Madrid and Valencia. Travel agents will have the latest information on flights and packages. Ibiza's modern airport has all the usual facilities for servicing international passengers. There is a regular bus service into Eivissa and a taxi ride costs around 1,300 pesetas.

Trasmediterránea's large ferry boats connect Eivissa with Palma de Mallorca, Barcelona and Valencia; they also take vehicles. Flebasa operate *rápidos* (hydrofoils) between Denia and both Eivissa and Sant Antoni. Ferries Pitiusos have connections between Gandia and both Eivissa and Formentera. Cruise liners call at Eivissa during the summer months.

Documents

Everyone must have a valid passport for entry into Spain. EU citizens can enter with a passport or a valid identity card. Countries such as the United States and Latin America do not need visas for stays of up to 90 days. Consult the Spanish Consulate in your country for updated information. Medical certificates are not usually required. But again check if in doubt.

I would not travel without an insurance policy which provides substantial cover for medical expenses due to ill health or accident. Driving licences issued by EU countries can be used by visitors to Spain. Visitors from other countries should have an International Driver's Permit.

Make photocopies of the front pages of your passport, as well as pages with any relevant visa stamps, your Travel Insurance policy, any medical prescriptions you have and your driving licence and keep them on your person together with a note of the name and telephone number of a person to contact in case of emergency. Keep original documents and a note of your credit card and travellers' cheque numbers in a secure place. I have regretted not following my own advice.

Customs Regulations

These are generally in line with other EC countries. Airlines, travel agents, the Spanish Tourist Office and Consulate can advise.

Money Matters

The peseta is issued in 10,000, 5,000, 2,000, 1,000 notes and 500, 200, 100, 50, 25, 10, 5 and 1 coins. Coins of 25 and 100 pesetas are the most useful for parking meters, telephones and slot machines.

All the major credit and charge cards are widely accepted; Visa the most so. And there are many cashpoints at which cards can be used with PINs. Banks, which are plentiful, are the best places to change currency. They open Monday to Friday 8.30am–2pm.

Electricity

Usuallly this is 220 Volts AC through two-pin round plugs. Bathrooms and a few older buildings may still have 110 Volt supplies. Adaptors are widely available.

ACCOMMODATION

Hotels are officially rated from one to five stars. *Hostals* have one to three stars. More basic are *Fondas* (Inns) and *Casas de Huéspedes* (Guest Houses). Officially classified Tourist Apartments (ATS) have one to three keys. Ibiza also has *Clubs de Vacaciones* (Holiday Clubs) and four camping sites. Much of the available accommodation in villas and apartments is not classified.

A good contact for villa rental is Ibiza House Renting, Plaza del Parque Eivissa, 07800, tel: 30 05 12; fax: 30 51 79. Official ratings of establishments relate to their physical amenities, staffing levels and such like. They say absolutely nothing about the hotel's ambience.

On Ibiza some of the most enchanting hostelries have few stars and some have no stars because their owners do not want classification. Rather than give a listing of hotels, which you can get at tourist offices, I will say a bit about my 10 favourites, including the grand, exotic, eccentric and humble establishments. Prices are high/low season; it is necessary to add on 7 percent IVA tax.

In Eivissa

ROYAL PLAZA
Calle Pedro Francés 27
Tel: 31 00 00
4-star Hotel Residencia
Opened in 1980, this is the biggest and priciest hotel in town. Rooms, most with balconies, and bathrooms are functionally appointed, the hotel is well-run and the front desk staff are noticeably efficient. Among the amenities is a rooftop swimming pool, a bar and restaurant.
Suite 38,500/21,600 pesetas.
Double 20,600/11,900 pesetas.

MOLINS PARK
Calle Joan Xico 42
Tel: 30 04 64
3-star Hostal Residencia
A 1990 addition to Eivissa's hotel panoply, it has only 30 rooms, all with balconies, which like their bathrooms are compact but well equipped. Like the Royal Plaza it attracts the island's business visitors.
Double 13,230/9,240 pesetas.

MONTESOL
Paseo Vara del Rey 2
Tel: 31 01 61
1-star Hotel Residencia
Situated in the attractive colonial style building above the café-bar of the same name, it is at the centre of the town's action. There is nothing fancy here, the attraction is the cost, situation and the amalgam of guests.
Double (bath) 7,250/5,473 pesetas.

EL CORSARIO
Calle Poniente 5, Dalt Vila
Tel: 30 12 48
2-star Hostal Residencia
Fourteen rooms of varying comfort are scattered around this dated conversion of a 17th-century mansion in the higher reaches of Dalt Vila. I have enjoyed sojourns in the room where Onassis and other luminaries are said to have cavorted over the years. Soundproofing and plumbing are not of the best, ancillary services are minimal but the attention is personal. Eccentric and charming. Open all year
Double: low season 8,000, mid-season 10,000, high season 12,000. Suite: low season 16,000; mid-season18,000; high season 20,000.

LA VENTANA
Sa Carrossa 13, Dalt Vila
Tel: 30 15 48
In 1984 a three-storey town house was converted into this charming *hostal*

which is now under the management of Philip Moseby. Of its 14 rooms the best are those with bathroom (not shower) and balcony looking across Sa Carrossa to the walls and bastions. The restaurant (open in winter for lunch and dinner, in summer for dinner only) is also recommended.
Double 22,000/16,000.

Out of Town

HACIENDA
Na Xamena, Port de Sant Miquel
Tel: 33 45 00
5-star Hotel
The only 5-star hotel in the Pine Islands fully deserves its stars and its Relais & Chateaux appointment. Magnificently placed upon a clifftop and surrounded by pine trees, the hotel is a cluster of low whitewashed buildings. Among the amenities are two outdoor pools, a heated indoor pool, tennis courts and boutiques. Some of the 53 rooms and 10 suites have jacuzzis. Both the poolside and indoor restaurants are of the gourmet standard demanded by Relais & Chateaux. Closed from end October to 26 April but opens, at high season rates, from 20 December–7 January.
Double 34,500/21,900 pesetas.
Top suite 41,800/28,600 pesetas.
Junior suite 36,000/24,500 pesetas.

TENNIS SPORT CENTRE HOTEL VILLAGE
Cala d'en Real, Sant Josep.
Tel: 80 00 34/80 80 01
Of striking modern design set around a swimming pool. Rooms and suites for only 40 guests who tend to be Spanish, German or French. There are four tennis courts, a gym and sauna, stairs to a secluded cove, a launch and skipper for hire and arrangements for other sports. Area to practise golf.
Double 24,500/18,500 pesetas (includes breakfast).

PIKE'S
Camí de Sa Vorera, Sant Antoni.
Tel: 34 22 22.
Forget about the 2-star *Hostal* rating: it reflects nothing of the ambience of relaxed sophistication which Tony Pike has over 10 years created among rambling and rustic pale yellow buildings in a peaceful countryside setting. Other stars – Julio Iglesias and George Michael – rate it as the 'best' and 'greatest' hotel in the world. Pike's has been the favourite place to stay of many entertainment stars who have come to Ibiza to perform at KU or just to unwind. English, enlivened by

An island institution

Tony's Australian twang, is generally the common tongue around the pool or for banter on the tennis court. Now has a new sports centre with pool, spa and Jacuzzi. The 26 very comfortable rooms and suites are all delightfully different in design and furnishings.
Double: 18,000 pesetas; mid-season 20,000; high season 25,000. Suite: low season 22,000; mid-season 28,000; high season 33,000. Deluxe suite: low season 60,000; mid-season 70,000; high season 90,000.

LES JARDINS DE PALERM
Sant Josep
Tel: 80 03 18
When Swiss René bought the old *finca* which had once been the home of an Italian pirate he had in mind a private place where he could entertain an international set of friends. It has become a dreamlike hideaway in luxuriant gardens and open to all – that is all who can afford it. Few of the rooms are the same but all are tastefully decorated; many have terraces; bathrooms are also well appointed. The laid-back and cosmopolitan socialising is centred on the romantic pool terrace with its bar and intimate restaurant to one side. Closed November to Easter.
Double in low season 17,000 pesetas. Suite in high season 40,000 pesetas.

C'AN BUFI
Near Siesta Urbanización
Santa Eulàlia
Tel: 33 00 16
1-star Hostal Residencia.
C'an Bufi runs a totally unpretentious hostelry in what was their family's home. The 17 bedrooms are functional and comfortable. It is the sort of place where you tell the cook you will be in or out for meals. To one side of the swimming pool is a shady arbour where barbecues are held in summer. Closed 15 January to 15 March.
Double 8,000 pesetas; single 6,500 pesetas; includes breakfast.

GETTING AROUND
Car and Bike Hire

Car hire is relatively expensive compared with Spain's mainland resort areas. The biggest local operator is Autos Ibiza/Betacar/Europcar whose head office is at Autos Ibiza, Carretera Aeropuerto km 6.3, Eivissa 07830, tel: 39 68 44. They have numerous offices throughout the islands, some of which also rent mopeds and motorbikes. Autos Isla Blanca, Calle Antoni Jaume, Eivissa, tel: 31 54 07, is another large local operator with several offices. Also at the airport is Avis Airport, tel: 80 91 76, and, in town, Avis Eivissa, tel:

and sharp corners add to the risks. Not drinking and driving, being careful, anticipating the stupidity of others and keeping your cool is about the best advice I can give. Car hire firms should tell you what to do in case of an accident or breakdown.

31 31 63. Paco Valentín, Calle Vicente Ramón 19, tel: 31 08 22, a smaller operator, has better prices, as does Autos Ribas, Vicente Cueruo, 3, Eivissa, tel: 30 18 11. Remember that insurance costs and 15 per cent VAT add considerably to the quoted prices. Some airlines have 'fly-drive' packages. In travel pages of newspapers in your country there may be companies advertising budget car rentals on the island, I have used some satisfactorily.

It is easy to rent mopeds, ordinary and off-roaders, in the resorts. The latter are handy for getting to some of the more isolated beaches and rural spots. On Formentera bicycles are a much favoured form of transport. If your holiday insurance excludes cover when using mopeds etc, get local insurance. The rules of the road are much the same as in the rest of Western Europe but Spain suffers from a much higher than average road accident and death rate, and Ibiza has one of Spain's highest per capita accident rates. Excess alcohol in drivers' bloodstreams is much of the explanation. Eccentric driving by local and foreign drivers is a hazard. Many foreigners are in high holiday mood; many British are not used to driving on the right; some locals, used to empty roads for much of the year, do not adjust to the greatly increased volume of traffic in summer. Dreaming or drunk pedestrians and motorcyclists, straying animals, farm vehicles lacking lights, narrow roads

If you are in your own car, your travel or car insurance may give instructions and provide for special arrangements. You may need to get a *grua* (tow truck) and find a *taller* (repair shop). *Gasolineras* (petrol stations) sell *normal* (92 octane), *super* (96), *gas-oil* (diesel) and more *sin plomo* (lead-free). Normal hours are 7am–10pm; 24-hour stations are at Es Tramuntana, Carretera Eivissa–Portinatx km1.7 and (with automatic cash payment machines) the petrol stations at Carretera Eivissa–Aeropuerto km1.7 and at the southern entrance to Santa Eulàlia.

Bus and Taxi

From in front of Eivissa's bus terminal at Avenida Isidoro de Macabich 44, and from No 24, there are regular daytime and early evening departures to and arrivals from Sant Antoni, Santa Eulàlia, the airport, Platja d'en Bossa, Las Salinas, Sant Joan and Cala Sant Vicent, Sant Miquel, Cala Llonga. Convenient stops are made at places en route. From Sant Antoni and Santa Eulàlia there are also regular connections with nearby beaches and tourist complexes.

Buses are cheap: for example, 155 pesetas from Eivissa to Sant Antoni. Taxis are relatively low-priced. Agree upon the fare in advance for longer journeys. There are fixed rates for most journeys. I always make a mental or written note of the taxi's permit number in case I leave something or there is a dispute. Telephone numbers of the *paradas* (taxi ranks) are: Eivissa 30 17 94; Airport 30 52 30; Figuertes 30 16 76; Sant Antoni 34 00 74; Santa Eulàlia 33 00 63; and on Formentera, Sa Savina 32 20 02, Es Pujols 32 80 16, St Francesc 32 20 16.

Ferry Services

Three operators of very regular ferry connections between Eivissa and Formentera are: Trasmapi (tel: 31 07 11); Inserco (tel: 31 11 55); Pitra (tel: 31 45 13), Flebasa (tel: 34 28 71); Marítima de Formentera (tel: 32 22 10). The terminal is on the west side of the port where fuller information is available; timetables can also be obtained from tourist offices and in local newspapers. Some boats take vehicles. Small boats regularly ply between Eivissa (near the Mallorca ferry terminal) and Talamanca and the marinas across the bay. There are also connections be-

tween Eivissa and Santa Eulàlia. From Santa Eulàlia ferries go to Es Canar, Cala Pada, S'Armagassa and Cala Llonga. The hotels around Sant Antoni's bay are served by ferries and there are services to the beaches of Port d'es Torrent, Cala Bassa, Cala Conta and Cala Tarida.

MEDIA & COMMUNICATION

Media

Diario de Ibiza is the local daily newspaper in Castilian. It also has a supplement in German and English during the summer months. There is also a monthly publication called *Ibiza Now*. Radio Ibiza-Ser operates on 98.1FM; Radio Diario de Ibiza on 102.8FM; Radio Popular de Ibiza on 89.1FM features English and German programmes at 9 and 10pm respectively. TVE 1 and TVE 2, Spain's two national television channels, give the best reception. Six

On the Formentera ferry

Post-box painter

other channels, public and private, are also available as well as a number of satellite programmes.

Communication

Post Offices (*Correos*) are open from 9am–2pm Monday to Friday and until 1pm on Saturday at Calle Madrid 23, Eivissa, tel: 31 13 80; Calle de la Mar s/n, Sant Antoni, tel: 34 07 79; Avenida Generalísimo 1, Santa Eulàlia, tel: 33 00 95; Plaza de la Constitució, Sant Francesc (Formentera), tel: 32 22 43. Telegrams can be sent from post offices or by telephone on 77 20 00. Mail, marked *Lista de Correos*, can be sent to you at the above post offices and an identity document is required when collecting. Hotels and commercial bureaux provide telex and fax services.

Telephone kiosks are plentiful and display instructions for use in a number of languages. To call other counries, first dial the international access code (7), then the relevant country code: Australia (61); France (33); Germany (49); Italy (39); Japan (81); Netherlands (31); United Kingdom (44 1); US and Canada (1). If you are using a US credit phone card, dial the company's access number below, the 01, and then the country code. Sprint, tel: 900 99 0013; AT&T, tel: 900 99 0011; MCI, tel: 900 99 0014.

EMERGENCIES

Police

The *Policia Nacional*, Tel: 091, deal with Spain's internal security and with law and order in the main urban areas. They have navy blue uniforms and their *comisaría* is on Avenida de la Pau, Tel: 30 53 13. They should be contacted in all cases of serious crime or in regard to immigration matters such as visa extensions. The *Guardia Civil* look after law and order along the coastline and in rural areas. They wear avocado green uniforms. Telephone numbers are: Eivissa 30 11 00; Sant Antoni 34 05 02; Santa Eulàlia 33 02 27; Sant Josep 80 00 24; Sant Joan 33 30 05; Formentera 32 24 68. The *Policia Local*, Tel: 092, also wearing blue but with check bands, are principally responsible for urban traffic control and civil protection. They also deal with lost property. Telephone numbers are: Eivissa 31 58 61; Sant Antoni 34 39 11; Santa Eulàlia 33 08 41; Sant Josep 80 02 61; Formentera 32 22 01.

Robbery

The islands have a very low rate of crime against visitors but it makes sense to take intelligent precautions, as you would anywhere, to deter rob-

beries from cars or private and hotel accommodation. There are infrequent muggings which are usually motivated by drug dependency. It is sensible to avoid dark, lonely streets and not to venture alone into the depths of Eivissa's Sa Penya quarter.

Accident and Sickness

If you have E110, E111 or E112 forms from your national health service, and are a resident of an EC country, you benefit from reciprocal arrangements with local health authorities. But I recommend all short-term visitors take out a travel insurance policy. A modern emergency and general hospital, Hospital Can Misses, is off the bypass on Eivissa's west side, tel: 39 70 00. Hotels, tourist offices and emergency services will assist with recommending or calling doctors.

The Red Cross (*Cruz Roja*) provides emergency attention and operates ambulances and sea rescue services: tel: 39 03 03; maritime division 39 03 03. Fire brigade (*bomberos*), tel: 31 30 30.

Pharmacies (*Farmacias*) are identified by green or red crosses and can often advise and deal directly with minor ailments. Outside normal shopping hours they display the name and address of the nearest open *farmacia de guardia*.

Consulates

The UK (tel: 30 18 18), Germany (tel: 31 57 63) and The Netherlands (tel: 30 04 50)have consulates in Eivissa. Many other countries have consulates in Palma de Mallorca. Police, tourist offices and hotels can provide addresses and telephone numbers.

USEFUL INFORMATION

Tourist Offices

Paseo Vara del Rey 13, **Eivissa**, tel: 30 19 00; Paseo de las Fuentes s/n, **Sant Antoni**, tel: 34 33 63; Calle María Riquer Wallis s/n, **Santa Eulàlia**, tel: 33 07 28; Port de Sa Savina, **Formentera**, tel: 32 20 57.

Sport

If sport is to be a significant interest in your holiday programme, you may want to consult with hotels and tourist offices by telephone, fax or mail in advance of your arrival. Permits are required for **sport and underwater fishing**. They are obtainable from the Consell Insular offices on Calle Besi, 9 (tel: 39 73 00), on weekday mornings. You need to take a copy of your passport and, for the underwater permit, a medical certificate.

There are **diving centres** offering instruction and equipment at Sant Antoni, Cala Vedella, Portinatx and on Formentera. You should have a proficiency certificate, your log book and a valid medical certificate.

Horses can be hired at **Can Mayans** (tel: 908 636 884), about 1km (½ mile) left off the road from Santa Gertrudis to Sant Llorenç. From these stables you can ride solo, with a guide, or in a group for a cost of around 2,000 pesetas per hour. Two other stables which offer much the same services as Can Mayans are: **Easy Rider**, Cala Llonga (tel: 33 91 92), located behind the line of buildings at the southern end; and **Can Sires** (tel: 34 15 54), near S'Olivera (follow signs to Pike's Hotel, on the right off the road between Sant Rafael and Sant Antoni).

Tennis players should bring their racquets to Ibiza. The **Ahmara Sport and Social Centre** has courts, some with floodlights (see *Pick & Mix* Option 4). Also, on the Eivissa–Sant Josep road, on the right just before Ahmara, is the **Club de Campo**, the island's top sport and social club, where you will have the opportunity of mixing with islanders. Another good option is Club Can Jordi, in Cala Llonga, which has plenty of tennis courts and an olympic-size swimming pool. **Club Fiestaland**, near Agualandia in Platja d'en Bossa, probably has the largest number of courts.

Golf: The **Ibiza Golf Club**, with 27 holes offers equipment and carts for hire, pro shops and the services of a professional. Green fees are around 6,000 pesetas. It is necessary to present your handicap card. For information and bookings contact: Club de Golf Ibiza, Santa Eulàlia, tel: 19 60 52.

Beaches and Waterparks

The Pine Islands have some of the cleanest beaches in the Mediterranean and annually receive a proportionately large number of Blue Flags from the EC environmental commission. On Ibiza my favourites are Las Salinas in the southeast and Cala d'en Sardina on the northwest coast (best reached by boat). On Formentera I prefer the sandy stretch of Platja de ses Illetes and the rocky shelves near Punta de sa Pedrera.

Waterparks provide an alternative to Ibiza's beaches. They usually offer facilities for greater bathing comfort and their installations provide thrilling slides and tumbles. Aguamar is in Platja d'en Bossa; Agualandia is at Cap Martinet past Talamanca. Their amenities include cafeterias or restaurants as well as picnic areas, solarium 'beaches', swimming 'lakes', changing rooms and showers, children's play areas, free-falling Kamikaze slides, and first aid stations. Both parks are open daily from 15 June to 15 September, 10am–6pm. Adults pay 1,600 pesetas, which covers all water activities; children pay half price.

ACKNOWLEDGMENTS

Photographer **Jens Poulsen** *and*
24, 38, 39, **Glyn Genin**
37 **Gary John Norman**
1, 29, 40B, 51, 53, 62B 70R, 90 **Bill Wassman**
Publisher **Hans Höfer**
Design Concept **V Barl**
Designer **Patrick Wong**
Layout **Erich Meyer**
Cover Design **Klaus Geisler**
Production Editor **Gareth Walters**
Cartography **Berndtson & Berndtson**